THE OPEN CHAMPIONSHIP
1998

OFFICIAL ANNUAL IN ASSOCIATION WITH

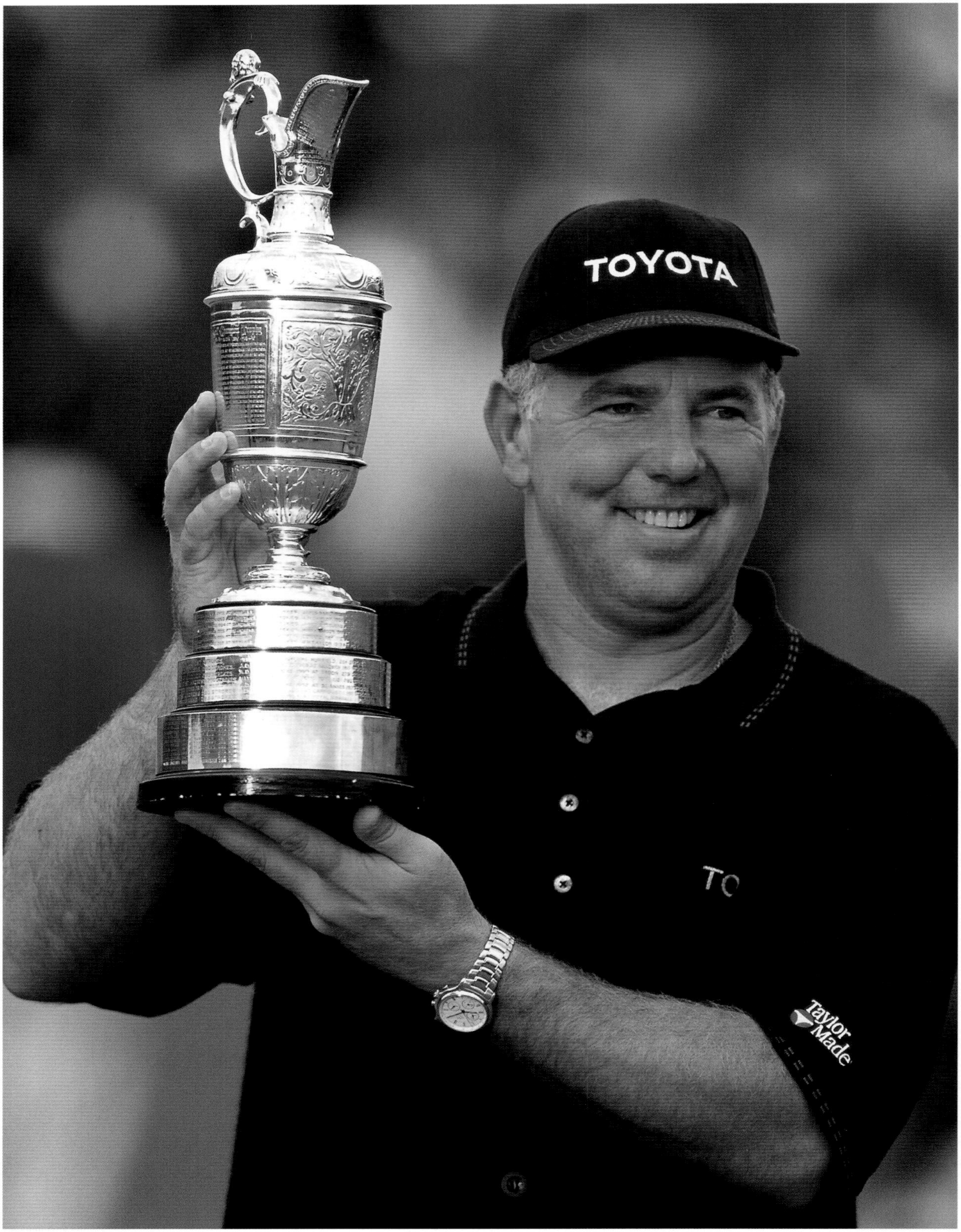
TOYOTA
TaylorMade

THE OPEN CHAMPIONSHIP
1998

OFFICIAL ANNUAL IN ASSOCIATION WITH

WRITERS

ROBERT SOMMERS
MICHAEL MCDONNELL
ROBERT GREEN
ANDREW FARRELL
ALISTER NICOL
JOHN HOPKINS

PHOTOGRAPHERS

MICHAEL COHEN
FRED VUICH

EDITOR

BEV NORWOOD

AUTHORISED BY THE
CHAMPIONSHIP COMMITTEE
OF THE ROYAL AND ANCIENT
GOLF CLUB OF ST ANDREWS

HAZLETON PUBLISHING LTD
3 Richmond Hill, Richmond, Surrey TW10 6RE

Published 1998 by Hazleton Publishing Ltd
Copyright © 1998 The Championship Committee Merchandising
Limited

Statistics of 127th Open Championship produced on a
Unisys Computer System

Course illustration courtesy of Elizabeth Peper

Fred Vuich is staff photographer for GOLF Magazine (USA)
and photographs are courtesy of Times Mirror Magazines, Inc.

Photographs on pages 12, 13, 15, 16 courtesy of Stephen Szurlej,
© The New York Times Company Magazine Group, Inc. All rights reserved.
Photographs on pages 36, 50 courtesy of Allsport Photographic Plc.

A CIP catalogue record for this book is available
from the British Library

ISBN: 1-874557-28-4

Typeset by Davis Design
Printed in Great Britain
by Butler & Tanner, Frome, Somerset

CONTENTS

INTRODUCTION

BY SIR RICHARD EVANS CBE
Chief Executive
British Aerospace plc

Once again, in 1998, the Open Championship provided us all with a feast of golf. The weather may have been disappointing for the spectators but it did serve to stiffen the unique challenges presented by the tremendous golf course at Royal Birkdale. In the end, we were treated to one of the most exciting finishes in recent years with a fine win by Mark O'Meara to add to his success at the Masters and a magnificent effort by the runner-up, Brian Watts.

An abiding memory for most of us will be the achievement of the young British amateur, Justin Rose, particularly his approach shot to make birdie on the 18th on the final day, which brought such a roar from the crowd. His performance coupled with his personal style epitomised everything that is good about the game of golf and I feel sure he will be the source of much inspiration for many young people about to take up the sport.

British Aerospace is proud to be the sponsor for National Golf Week, in conjunction with the PGA, which will provide opportunities for people from all walks of life to experience the pleasure of playing golf. We firmly believe that this is a very worthwhile initiative which will encourage many more people to take up the sport and share our enjoyment.

I would like to congratulate the Royal and Ancient Golf Club and the 1998 Championship Committee for staging such a tremendously successful event and look forward to 1999 when the Championship returns to Carnoustie in Scotland.

Sir Richard Evans CBE

THE CHAMPIONSHIP COMMITTEE

CHAIRMAN

H. M. CAMPBELL

DEPUTY CHAIRMAN

G. HUDDY

COMMITTEE

P. E. BECHMANN
R. M. BURNS
J. J. N. CAPLAN
P. J. HEDGES
A. J. HILL
R. D. JAMES
J. M. KIPPAX
A. J. N. LOUDON
M. S. R. LUNT
R. D. MUCKART
J. L. S. PASQUILL
N. M. STEPHENS

ADDITIONAL MEMBER

M. N. DOYLE
COUNCIL OF NATIONAL GOLF UNIONS

SECRETARY

SIR MICHAEL BONALLACK, OBE

CHAMPIONSHIP SECRETARY

D. HILL

ASSISTANT SECRETARY (CHAMPIONSHIPS)

D. R. WEIR

ASSISTANT SECRETARY (CHAMPIONSHIPS)

A. E. FARQUHAR

INTRODUCTION

BY H. M. CAMPBELL
Chairman of Championship Committee
Royal and Ancient Golf Club of St Andrews

With the varying wind and weather conditions, the Royal Birkdale golf course presented a formidable challenge for the strong international field who competed for the 127th Open Championship. The eighth Open Championship to be held at Royal Birkdale was certainly one of the most exciting. The excellence of Mark O'Meara's play was reflected in his scores of 72, 68, 72 and 68 for a level-par 280 aggregate.

The ability and courage of Brian Watts, less known at the beginning of the week, was also shown in his brave bunker shot on the 72nd hole to force a play-off. Tiger Woods excited his following with an effort that was one stroke too many, while Britain's own young Justin Rose won the Silver Medal in great style with the finest performance by an amateur since 1953.

Over 158,000 spectators for the four rounds of the Championship, plus 37,000 for the practice days, resulted in the best-attended Open ever at Royal Birkdale and the second-best in the history of the Championship.

The Royal and Ancient Championship Committee are very grateful for the support from the many sources necessary for a successful Championship, starting with the 15 Regional and four Final Qualifying Clubs, together with the Captain, Committee, Greenkeeper and Members of Royal Birkdale Golf Club, all of whom contributed significantly.

We also appreciate the continued support of British Aerospace for this official Annual, and we thank the photographers and writers whose work appears on the following pages.

H. M. Campbell

FOREWORD

BY MARK O'MEARA

The week of the Open Championship at Royal Birkdale was very, very special for me. It was just an incredible feeling to win this championship and to receive the trophy. When I look at the names of the past champions and the golf courses where they won, it is a tremendous honour to see my name alongside theirs.

What makes this championship so different and so special is that it is played on links courses, the way golf was started. Links golf really challenges and tests a player's ability. This week, with the fairways narrow and the rough deep, you had to drive the ball well. You had to create a lot of different shots with the winds — crosswinds, headwinds, downwinds. Variety is what golf is all about.

I felt if I played well and kept my composure, coming down the stretch hopefully I would have a chance to win. That's all you can ask in golf. There were lots of ups and downs out there, and the key was keeping my composure all week. I hit some poor shots but I didn't let that affect me mentally, and I made some putts at key moments when I needed to make them. I cannot say enough good about the other contenders, especially Brian Watts, Tiger Woods and the amateur Justin Rose, and it was an unforgettable experience to get the job done.

Mark O'Meara

Royal Birkdale's majestic sand dunes are evident on the sixth, par 4 and 480 yards, which proved to be the most difficult

hole in the 127th Open Championship.

ROUND ROYAL BIRKDALE

No. 1 449 Yards, Par 4

A stern warning of what lies ahead because the tee shot must be precisely placed on a fairway that sweeps left but then turns right towards a small well-protected green.

No. 2 421 Yards, Par 4

Another demanding tee shot to a fairway that bears left and requires an even more exact approach shot into the prevailing wind to a green that is flanked by bunkers.

No. 3 407 Yards, Par 4

The tee shot must favour the left side of the fairway for a better approach to the green which is set towards the right and requires accurate club selection because of the "dead" ground in front.

No. 4 203 Yards, Par 3

The longest of the short holes and, depending on wind strength and direction, may require considerable power as well as accuracy to carry the penal bunkers that surround the front of the green.

No. 5 344 Yards, Par 4

A dogleg to the right with water that menaces only the wildest shot. The green is narrow and heavily protected by bunkers, and birdie chances are reduced because of the subtle putting contours.

No. 6 480 Yards, Par 4

Play is dictated by the right-hand fairway bunker, which forces the tee shot left for a better line to an elevated green that is exposed to the elements and difficult to reach in two.

No. 7 177 Yards, Par 3

A new elevated tee 50 yards left of the original position means the shot is now played down the length of the green, but still presents difficulties because of wind changes and an array of greenside bunkers.

No. 8 457 Yards, Par 4

A range of right-hand fairway bunkers await the ill-considered drive, but even from a well-placed position the approach is extremely demanding to a large elevated green that is cleverly contoured.

No. 9 411 Yards, Par 4

The tee shot is blind and slightly uphill to the ridge of a right-hand doglegged fairway. The green is elevated and protected as much by crosswinds as the bunkers and heavy rough that surround it.

No. 10 403 Yards, Par 4

A sweeping dogleg to the left around sandhills, so the tee shot must be directed beyond the corner to allow clear sight of the green, which is set snugly into the dunes.

No. 11 408 Yards, Par 4

A raised tee makes the wind a formidable foe with bunkers either side of the landing area. Only one bunker guards the green, which falls away to the right and presents a very difficult target.

No. 12 183 Yards, Par 3

The green is framed neatly by sandhills but can be difficult to hit because of the swirling winds. The tee is also sheltered by dunes, which sometimes make club selection particularly hard.

No. 13 498 Yards, Par 4

Formerly a par-5, the reduction in length has brought the fairway bunkers into play because the tee shot should be aimed right to set up the ideal second shot to a green protected by the dunes.

No. 14 198 Yards, Par 3

The tee is elevated and set among sandhills and protected from the wind, which can cause problems once the shot moves across open terrain and into the crosswind. Correct club and line are essential.

No. 15 544 Yards, Par 5

The start of the long homeward stretch and, with the wind against, the main task is to find the fairway with first and second shots because of 13 bunkers between tee and green.

No. 16 416 Yards, Par 4

Heavy emphasis on the approach because the green is elevated and very small, so correct judgement of wind strength and direction is vital. A plaque commemorates Arnold Palmer's famous shot from a bush in the 1961 Open.

No. 17 547 Yards, Par 5

The tee has been moved left so that the drive between the sentinel dunes requires more accuracy and makes the hole play as a slight left-hand dogleg. The green is protected by sandhills but the entrance is narrowed by bunkers.

No. 18 472 Yards, Par 4

Another elevated tee with wind usually blowing left to right towards the out-of-bounds fence. The green is surrounded by bunkers, while others have been placed strategically along the fairway.

COMBINING OLD AND NEW VALUES

BY MICHAEL McDONNELL

When the distinguished Australian Peter Thomson was asked to define those qualities of a great championship course that set it apart from all others, he observed, "If there is just one tiny part of your game that is not quite right, the great course will find it out, no matter how hard you try to hide it."

The clear implication from the five times Open champion was that a great challenge must examine exhaustively every aspect of the game in terms of skill, strategy and personal character and in so doing reduce the list of candidates until only one — the champion — remains.

In such terms has Royal Birkdale scrutinised the ability of successive generations of outstanding international competitors to adapt to the specific demands of links golf and, in the broader context of the global sport, identify the truly complete golfer who can function at his best in whatever conditions he finds.

This is a giant of a course with breathtaking terrain and towering sandhills that offer the most majestic panoramic views of the Lancashire coastline stretching out towards the Irish Sea. For centuries this rolling terrain, hidden under willow scrub and bushes, was simply a golf course waiting to be discovered and not until 1889, when nine like-minded local enthusiasts decided to form themselves into a club and play the royal and ancient game, did its true destiny begin to emerge.

The combined design skills of J.H. Taylor and Fred Hawtree transformed the course in 1933 to provide a route through and between the sandhills rather than over them, thus eliminating as many blind shots as possible. Consequently, when Lee Trevino took his first look at Royal Birkdale from Waterloo Road

Arnold Palmer's plaque on the 16th.

before the 1971 championship he perceived nothing but sandhills and observed, "Man, this is moon country."

In fact the Taylor-Hawtree design had produced a relatively level playing surface on most fairways, which consequently removed much of the random fortune that is regarded as a traditional characteristic of links golf. In a sense, therefore, Royal Birkdale has been able to combine both old and new values, and over the years allow contrasting styles of play and philosophy to co-exist and reap equal rewards.

In 1965 Thomson was regarded as a figure from the past who had given way to the modern power era, personified by Jack Nicklaus and Arnold Palmer. Yet the courtly Australian found a judicious way round Royal Birkdale that owed much to his judgement and ability to play to specific points on every fairway and in so doing take the hazards out of play. It was a performance of such high quality that it could not be matched and he became champion for the fifth time.

Yet, only four years earlier at Birkdale, Palmer had continued his restoration of the Open Championship in particular, and the game of golf in general, with an heroic display that defied the savage elements and established him as a major figure on both sides of the Atlantic.

In actual terms Arnold disproved the legendary Walter Hagen's axiom about winning in golf that: "It's not how. It's how many." With Arnie, the manner of winning was all-important, particularly to his fans, and became as much part of their perception of him as the huge scale of his success.

In the 1961 Open he struck defiant form in the teeth of a gale that brought down several huge tents

The relatively flat fairways of Royal Birkdale run through dunes, willow scrub and buckhorn.

and sent scores soaring into the 80s on the second day. Incredibly, Arnold had five birdies in the first six holes and treated the tempest with complete disdain. But there were other moments too that contributed to his legend.

He called a penalty stroke on himself because his ball moved in a bunker as he was about to play. Nobody else saw it. But Arnold did. And later he made the famous six-iron escape from a bush that put the ball on the green and kept him in the lead and on his way to his first Open and a pilgrimage that every aspiring golfer thereafter followed.

Thus, two contrasting styles — and totally opposing philosophies on the game — have found success at Royal Birkdale because both campaigners were united in their fulsome respect for its challenge and never once lost serious focus.

Ironically, Trevino allowed his concentration to lapse at a crucial moment in 1971, and feared he might have ruined a remarkable run during which he had won the US Open and the Canadian Open in the previous weeks and seemed destined to take the Open title until a wayward drive from the 17th tee in the final round threw his hopes into deep crisis.

The ball landed on a high bank of willow scrub and he could only hack towards the green. Had his Taiwanese playing partner and closest rival Lu Liang Huan, nicknamed "Mister Lu," had a little more

power to get home with his second shot, the outcome might have been different. As it was, Super Mex took 7 but still held a one-stroke lead and went on to win his third title in four weeks.

It was an outstanding performance and one which underlined the truth of Nicklaus' tribute after Trevino had beaten him a play-off for the US Open title at Merion a few weeks earlier, "If Lee ever realises just how good he really is, we had all better watch out."

By the time Tom Watson scored his fifth title in 1983, the Open was clearly established as the most international event in the world calendar, attracting nearly all the best golfers who were qualified to play. He timed his winning run to perfection that year by taking the lead with one round to play then fending off all threats with a superlative two iron into the final green to ensure a one-stroke victory.

He was then set for a possible hat trick of successive titles a year later at St Andrews, but was to be thwarted by his own misjudgement on the Road Hole and more significantly by the efforts of Severiano Ballesteros, who went on to become Open champion in dramatic style.

The world at large first caught a glimpse of Ballesteros in 1976 at Royal Birkdale when, as a raw 19-year-old farmer's son, he led the Open for three rounds by carving a wayward route that neither Taylor nor Hawtree could ever have imagined for

The fifth green is narrow and heavily protected by bunkers.

The par-3 12th green is framed neatly by sandhills but can be difficult to reach.

The tee shot at the 13th should be aimed right to set up the ideal second shot to the green.

their masterpiece. It simply could not last but it almost did.

Johnny Miller, the eventual champion, played with brilliant flair to finish with 66 to edge past the wildly talented young Spaniard, who played an exquisite chip shot on the last hole that brought the delighted fans to their feet and earned him a share of second place with Nicklaus.

There were familiar echoes this year as 17-year-old Justin Rose delighted the world with his intrepid performance amongst the stars and gave the hint of things to come. Indeed the judgement offered by Miller on Ballesteros all those years ago has some topical relevance.

Miller said then, "It is good for him that he did not win the Open at such a young age. The expectations on him would have been too great. He will do it in his own time." Three years later, Seve was the champion.

Royal Birkdale has never witnessed such spectacular scoring in an Open as the 29 strokes over the outward nine holes of the 1991 championship with which Ian Baker-Finch separated himself from his rivals and left them with no chance of catching him as he went on to become champion.

It was fitting compensation for the agonies of his past near-misses and, though we never suspected at the time, would eventually provide a golden reminder in the dark hours that lay ahead in his career, that he was once rightfully esteemed as an outstanding player of world class.

In truth, this famous golf course has become a global theatre for high drama, monumental achievement and rare moments of history. The memory still endures of Nicklaus and Tony Jacklin, arms round each other's shoulders, marching from the last green after the 1969 Ryder Cup match between Great Britain and Ireland and the United States had been tied because of Jack's sportsmanship.

Jacklin faced a very missable putt on which the entire contest depended. It was a crushing responsibility, especially after three days of glorious and even combat. Nicklaus decided the putt was unnecessary and conceded it saying, "I didn't think you would miss it. But I wasn't going to give you the chance."

It was a truly noble gesture that ignored the win-at-all-costs mentality that often robs sport of its essential joy and instead upheld wider values of correctness and fair play. Nicklaus had underlined the enduring principle on which golf must exist: How the game is played matters more than how well it is played. That, too, will always be the legacy of Royal Birkdale.

The 16th green is elevated and very small, so correct judgement of wind is vital.

The par-5 17th yielded 27 eagles and 196 birdies, by far the most of any hole.

John Huston played the second nine in 31, having four birdies and an eagle, for his 65 to share the first-round lead.

LOW SCORES ON A MILD DAY

BY ROBERT SOMMERS

No one knew quite what to expect when the 127th Open Championship came to Royal Birkdale. Those who had played in previous Birkdale Opens could be sure only that the course would play differently, because so much effort had been put into rebuilding every one of its greens, digging out layers of muck that had given them a spongy texture, lengthening some holes, and re-positioning tees on others.

The greens putted much better than they had in 1991, Royal Birkdale's last previous Open, and for most of the week the wind saw to it that length didn't matter much. Where the sixth, a mean par-4 hole of 480 yards, asked the players to use very long clubs for their second shots, the 17th, which measured 547 yards, could be reached with medium-iron seconds. When the wind was up, par didn't matter much.

Tales of horror circulated even before the championship began. Playing a practice round on a windy day early in the week, Ernie Els, one of the longest hitters in the game, complained that with the sixth playing into the wind he needed a driver and three wood to reach the green.

Playing the 16th, a par-4 of 416 yards, Robert Allenby, a 27-year-old Australian, hit a driver and three iron and didn't make the green. He admitted he should have played a two iron. Lee Janzen, who had won the US Open a month earlier, hit the same clubs and made the green, although he said his drive didn't reach the fairway. Janzen also lost five balls, and Tom Lehman, the 1996 Open champion, lost six balls in eight holes.

It was different on the downwind holes. Playing the eighth, which measured 457 yards, Mark O'Meara hit his one iron 338 yards, and Tiger Woods drove the ball more than 450 yards. On the previous hole, though, a 177-yard par-3 into the wind, Woods hit a three iron 152 yards. On a calm day he can hit a nine iron farther.

The players commented also that they had to play wide of their targets and allow crosswinds to bring the ball back into play. Janzen said, "Sometimes you have to aim 20 yards off the fairway just to get the ball back into play." In America, he said, you might aim to the edge of the fairway.

Putting, too, was at risk. Els said he would have to be very careful putting downwind, downhill and down-grain. "Same with the other way," he added. "Going into the wind, you give it a good whack."

Of course, the weather played tricks once the championship opened. When the early starters arrived to warm up at about 6.00, they found the gale winds had died down, the sun shining, and Royal Birkdale altogether benign. Every green was in reach, and drives on the dreaded sixth left the players within 180 to 200 yards of the green. Indeed, Royal Birkdale played so much easier than anyone expected that 27 men shot in the 60s, 14 others matched par 70, and 88 of the 156 starters shot 72 or less. The course would never play so easy again.

Woods had been a disappointment at Royal Troon the previous year, but here he bounced back with an opening round of 65, which would have led the 1991 Open but earned Tiger no more than a tie for first place. John Huston, a 37-year-old American who had never placed higher than a tie for 31st in his previous four Opens, shot 65 as well.

Nick Price, Fred Couples and Loren Roberts, all old Open hands, shot 66s; five others shot 67; 10 more 68, and seven others 69. Davis Love III, the 1997 USPGA Championship winner, was among those at 67. Jesper Parnevik, the Swede who had come so close at Turnberry in 1994 and at Royal Troon in 1997, shot 68, the same as Brian Watts, an American who plays in Japan.

Meantime, Justin Leonard, who had made up five strokes in the last round and won at Royal Troon, shot 73, along with Severiano Ballesteros, John Daly,

Jean Louis Guepy of France had the honour to start the 127th Open Championship.

Nick Price (66) had "a really good start."

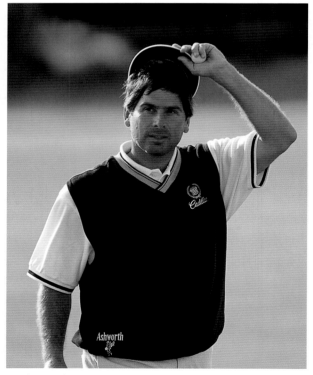

Fred Couples (66) made an eagle 3 on the 15th hole.

Loren Roberts (66) birdied two of the first three holes.

Jose Maria Olazabal, Tom Watson and Colin Montgomerie. David Duval shot 70. Lee Westwood shot 71, along with Lehman, Payne Stewart, Sandy Lyle, Phil Mickelson and Stewart Cink. O'Meara, Janzen, Els, Nick Faldo and Ian Woosnam each shot 72.

Americans held six of the first 10 places. The one European in that group was Fredrik Jacobson, a 23-year-old Swede in his first Open Championship, with his 67 including an eagle 3 on the 17th. Bothered for several months early in the year by a torn ligament in his left thumb, Jacobson had missed the 36-hole cut in seven of his 13 European events of 1998.

Of the current European leaders, Westwood had the best start, sharing 42nd place for the first round with his 71.

Montgomerie's 73 was the most disappointing score of all. He had said before that he saved his worst golf for the third week in July, and indeed he did once again. Seeing his position in the standings, he moaned, "All I've got left is trying to make the cut."

Of the leaders, Huston was off first, starting at 8.35, grouped with Cink, another American, and Toru Taniguchi, from Japan.

Hardly more than a journeyman professional, with

A smiling Tiger Woods (65) went out in 30.

23

Sweden's Fredrik Jacobson (67) was low European.

Brad Faxon (67) had his best putting of the year.

four career victories since 1983, Huston was, nevertheless, having a good year. He had won the United Airlines Hawaiian Open, tied for second at the Doral-Ryder Open in Miami, for fifth in the BellSouth Classic in Atlanta and for eighth in the Phoenix Open. Still, he had not done much in either the Masters, where he tied for 23rd, or the US Open, where he tied for 32nd. In those two tournaments he had shot as low as 70 only in the third round of the Masters.

Like some other golfers, Huston has his quirks, not quite so bizarre as Parnevik's eating volcanic sand, but he does carry a special mattress cover filled with tiny magnets sewn into the fabric. The magnets are said to increase the flow of blood and ease the pain of tendinitis in his right wrist and bursitis in his left shoulder.

"I had a permanent dull ache," he said, "and when I woke up I didn't want to go to work."

Then a stranger who had heard of Huston's affliction approached him in the carpark of a club in Palm Springs, California, a year and a half earlier and promised him a cure. He gave him a magnetised mattress cover.

"Does it work?" he was asked. A realist, he answered, "It seems to work for those who think it works."

Huston opened with a ragged first hole, where he holed from 25 feet to save his par 4, but then he ran off eight more pars and turned for home in 34, level par for Birkdale's first nine. Not bad, but he would have to do something better on such a mild day. Then, suddenly, Huston birdied four holes coming in, eagled another, bogeyed one, shot 31, and jumped to the top of the leaderboard. His iron play was

Davis Love III (67) had several loose drives.

Vijay Singh (67) made eagle at the 17th.

Robert Allenby (67) played without a bogey.

inspiring. He played his approaches to 10 feet on the 10th, 12 feet on the 11th, hit his tee shot to eight feet on the 12th, played a 215-yard seven iron from the rough to four feet on the 18th and birdied them all. Playing the 17th downwind, Huston reached the green with a three wood and six iron and holed from 40 feet for the eagle 3, one of seven on that hole that day.

Huston agreed Birkdale was a totally different course from what he had seen in his practice rounds, when he thought a score of 290, 10 over par, might win the Open. Now, though, he planned nothing more than enjoying the day, because, "Who knows what the weather is going to be tomorrow?"

Woods and O'Meara had planned intelligently for the Open. Knowing they would be exposed to an unfamiliar type of golf, they toured Ireland for a week and played two links courses, Ballybunion and Waterville, and the K Club. It paid off.

While Huston shot his 65 before only a few spectators, a usual and enthusiastic throng trotted after Woods. Tiger gave them a series of thrills. Showing how well he had prepared, he streaked out in 30, four under par, but it had been a nervous start.

He missed the first green and saved his par by holing from eight feet, then drove into a bad lie in deep rough on the second. "It was a horrible place," Woods said. "One of those lies that might mean you only move the ball four feet."

Woods lashed into the shot, the ball flew out, soared over a bunker, and carried 120 yards to the green. Another par was saved.

Now he made his move. Driving with a five iron on the third, a 407-yard hole, he pitched to 10 feet, played a two iron and nine iron to 12 feet on the

David Howell (68) was three under on the second nine.

It was another disappointing Open start for Colin Montgomerie (73), who had 40 on the second nine.

Lee Westwood (71) hoped to putt better.

fifth, hit a five iron to the back edge of the seventh, a par-3, and holed all three putts.

Now he approached the ninth, a par-4 of 411 yards that doglegs right, around a high dune that masks a hidden bunker. He had delighted his followers by trying to drive the green during practice rounds, but said later that he wouldn't try so risky a shot during the Open itself. Still, the spectators wondered.

Woods was playing with Price, who had a good round going as well, and since Nick had birdied the eighth, he had the honour on the ninth tee. When the gallery saw a ball bounce off the side of the dune and settle about 260 yards out, they figured Tiger had put his driver away once more and driven with an iron. Of course, that was Price's ball. Minutes later another ball tore over the dune, hit at the spectators' crosswalk, which, mercifully, was empty, and rolled on towards the green. After realising what they had seen, the fans roared.

Asked about the decision to play so dangerous a shot, Woods said, "To me it makes no sense to lay up when I can carry that bunker. There is no rough down there on the right, and the left rough is really thin. I hit a normal driver today, without killing it,

Philip Walton (68) posted six birdies.

Andrew Coltart (68) made eagle at the 15th.

and got it up into the wind. That was the key to it; get it airborne and let it ride the wind."

The ball had rolled within 20 yards of the green, and Tiger had only a sand wedge left. He pitched to six feet and struck a bold putt into the cup. Out in 30, he lost a stroke at the 12th when another bold putt caught a corner of the hole and spun away, but he birdied the 13th, at 498 yards the longest par-4 on record. Distance meant nothing to Woods. He drove with a two iron, reached the green with a six-iron second, and holed from 30 feet.

Still four under par, he had two par-5s coming up and could match Royal Birkdale's record first-round score of 64, set by Craig Stadler in 1983, or perhaps Jodie Mudd's 63 of 1991, the lowest score for any round.

At the 15th, a 544-yard par-5 playing into the wind, Woods reached the edge of the green with a drive and two iron and birdied. He had an easier time on the downwind 17th, reaching the green with a three wood and six iron to 30 feet. His first putt went 12 feet past the hole but he made that for yet another birdie. Six under now, a par 4 on the 18th and he would shoot 64.

After another glorious drive, Woods played an eight iron that skipped over the green, followed with an indifferent chip to eight feet, and he bogeyed.

Price had watched Tiger's entire round, of course, and spoke of his restraint. He said that whereas in the past Woods might play every shot for all it was worth, he had throttled back and had gone flat out only with his two iron into the 15th. Lying 240 yards from the green, he had rifled his shot six or seven yards past the hole.

"A year ago," Price suggested, "he wouldn't have been able to resist hitting a whole lot of shots like that."

As another sign of his maturing game, Woods used his driver on only four holes.

Price hasn't done much to distinguish himself since winning the 1994 USPGA Championship, but he feels he is still improving. Always a superb ball-striker, Nick has his greatest problems on the greens. He claimed he's a mediocre putter 70 percent of the time, but he had worked to improve. He had switched from a blade to a mallet-headed putter two weeks earlier and worked on his putting two or three hours a day, "as long as my back would allow."

Perhaps it worked, because Price putted beautifully in the first round. After losing a stroke at the

Ian Woosnam (72) took 6 on the par-4 13th.

first, Price holed from 15 feet on the third, from 22 feet on the fifth, and from 12 feet on the eighth, the kind he called "bonus putts."

Two under par on the first nine, he gave up another stroke on the 10th where he misjudged the speed of his first putt, left it 12 feet short, and missed. Quickly, though, he struck back, holed from 20 feet on the 12th, a par-3, then birdied both the 15th and 17th. A driver and three wood left him just short of the 15th green, but he chipped to four feet and made the putt, then reached the 17th green with a driver and six iron and got down in two from 35 feet. Back in 34, he shot 66 to be one stroke off the lead.

"It was really a good start," Price said later. "Just the two bogeys, which I'm a little upset about. They were the only two greens I missed. I'm striking the ball pretty well and I putted solidly."

Couples played steady golf with only two lapses. Three under par after the 13th, which he birdied, Fred missed a three-foot putt on the 14th, his first error. An eagle 3 on the 15th dropped him to four under par, with the 17th coming up. Couples, though, hooked his drive into deep rough on a hillside and fought to make his par 5. Still, with 66, he too stood just one stroke off the lead.

Leonard and Montgomerie, on the other hand, were left wondering if they would survive the 36-hole cut. With 73s, both knew they would have to improve if they hoped to play the last two rounds.

Leonard's driving, usually steady, periodically put him in difficult positions. He had to struggle on the fifth, eighth, 13th and 18th holes. He started well enough with two birdies and two bogeys through the first 10 holes, but he pushed his drive into high grass on the 13th, slashed a wedge shot perhaps 80 yards into more rough, yanked his third across the fairway into still more rough, and made 6.

"I'm very disappointed to shoot three over par on a day when there are very good scores. You don't expect to have good lies in the rough, but in the practice rounds I had been able to get a few out. Twice today I tried to play a sand wedge out and I wasn't able to. But it's my fault for hitting it in there."

The gallery was standing 10 deep around the first tee at 9.05, waiting to cheer on Montgomerie. For a time the support seemed to work, and it looked like he might shake off the jinx that had haunted him in nearly every Open he had played.

Montgomerie has said that when he putts well he usually wins. It looked promising at the third, where he holed a downhill 15-footer for one birdie, then ripped a three iron within six feet on the difficult sixth for another. A stroke was lost on the seventh, where he missed the green, and he was out in 33, one under par.

Suddenly the strokes began slipping away. Normally the straightest of drivers with his controlled fade, Montgomerie began hooking the ball, lost one stroke at the 12th, another when he drove into a bunker on the 13th, still another at the 16th where he bunkered his approach shot, and one more when he pulled his approach into the left rough on the 18th. He had finished with four consecutive 5s, two of them pars, come back in 40 and seriously damaged his confidence.

"The fade has gone," he said, "and now I hook the ball. I'm afraid in a right-to-left wind … Obviously I was disappointed … To finish with four 5s isn't very good. But there's always tomorrow, I suppose."

Five-times champion Tom Watson (73) said he "did not keep the ball in play enough."

Ernie Els (72) took double bogey on the sixth.

Nick Faldo (72) made pars on both par 5s.

FIRST ROUND RESULTS

HOLE	1	2	3	4	5	6	7	8	9	10	11	12	13	14	15	16	17	18	TOTAL
PAR	4	4	4	3	4	4	3	4	4	4	4	3	4	3	5	4	5	4	TOTAL
John Huston	4	4	4	3	4	4	3	4	4	3	3	2	4	4	5	4	3	3	65
Tiger Woods	4	4	3	3	3	4	2	4	3	4	4	4	3	3	4	4	4	5	65
Nick Price	5	4	3	3	3	4	3	3	4	5	4	2	4	3	4	4	4	4	66
Fred Couples	3	4	4	3	4	4	3	4	4	4	3	3	3	4	3	4	5	4	66
Loren Roberts	4	3	3	3	4	4	3	5	4	4	4	2	4	3	4	4	4	4	66
Fredrik Jacobson	4	4	4	3	5	4	3	5	3	4	3	2	4	3	4	5	3	4	67
Brad Faxon	5	4	3	3	4	4	3	3	3	4	5	2	5	3	5	3	4	4	67
Davis Love III	4	4	3	3	4	4	4	4	4	3	3	3	4	3	4	3	5	4	67
Vijay Singh	4	3	3	3	4	4	3	4	4	4	3	3	4	3	5	4	3	5	67
Robert Allenby	4	4	4	3	4	3	2	4	4	4	4	3	4	3	5	4	4	4	67
David Howell	4	5	4	3	4	4	3	4	4	5	3	2	5	2	3	4	4	5	68
Stephen Ames	5	4	3	3	4	4	3	4	3	4	4	3	3	4	4	4	5	4	68
Bob Tway	4	4	3	4	4	5	3	4	3	4	4	3	3	4	4	4	5	4	68
Greg Turner	4	4	4	3	4	5	2	4	3	4	5	3	4	3	4	3	4	5	68
Jesper Parnevik	3	4	4	3	4	4	4	3	3	4	4	3	4	3	5	4	5	4	68
Philip Walton	3	5	3	2	4	4	3	4	4	5	5	2	4	3	4	4	4	5	68
Thomas Bjorn	4	4	4	3	4	4	3	4	3	4	3	3	4	4	4	4	5	4	68
Raymond Russell	4	4	4	3	4	5	4	3	4	4	3	3	4	3	4	3	4	4	68
Brian Watts	5	4	3	3	4	4	3	5	5	3	3	3	4	3	4	4	4	4	68
Andrew Coltart	4	4	4	3	4	5	2	4	4	5	4	3	4	3	3	3	5	4	68

HOLE SUMMARY

HOLE	PAR	EAGLES	BIRDIES	PARS	BOGEYS	HIGHER	RANK	AVERAGE
1	4	0	9	76	63	8	1	4.47
2	4	0	16	109	29	2	8	4.12
3	4	0	22	103	31	0	10	4.06
4	3	0	24	108	22	2	15	3.01
5	4	1	19	109	25	2	12	4.05
6	4	0	11	77	60	8	3	4.42
7	3	0	15	117	24	0	10	3.06
8	4	0	20	115	18	3	14	4.03
9	4	0	26	100	28	2	13	4.04
OUT	34	1	162	914	300	27		35.26
10	4	0	7	119	26	4	6	4.18
11	4	0	21	93	35	7	5	4.19
12	3	0	21	114	20	1	16	3.01
13	4	0	17	79	49	11	4	4.35
14	3	0	13	117	25	1	9	3.10
15	5	4	43	94	13	2	17	4.78
16	4	0	18	105	29	4	7	4.12
17	5	7	58	78	11	2	18	4.64
18	4	0	8	81	57	10	2	4.46
IN	36	11	206	880	265	42		36.83
TOTAL	70	12	368	1794	565	69		72.09

Players Below Par	27
Players At Par	14
Players Above Par	115

LOW SCORES

Low First Nine	Tiger Woods	30
Low Second Nine	John Huston	31
Low Round	John Huston	65
	Tiger Woods	65

WEATHER

Temperature: low 15°C, high 25°C.
Moderate west to southwest wind.

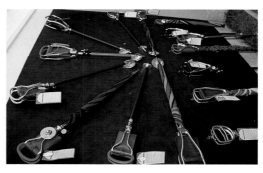

Tiger Woods described Royal Birkdale as "extremely difficult but it is fair. All the trouble is right in front of you."

HORRIFIC SLUMPS AND SURPRISES

BY ROBERT GREEN

It has become a quasi-tradition of the Open Championship that the first-round leader is a comparative unknown. This year, that was only the case if you were a Martian.

A six-under-par 65 propelled Tiger Woods, officially ranked the No. 1 player in the game, to the top of the leaderboard at the conclusion of the first day's play at Royal Birkdale. This was, of course, a surprise. Agreed, technically Tiger might have been the world No. 1, but then everyone knew he was mired in such a horrific slump that he had only won twice this year — indeed, only won twice since he played in his first Open Championship as a professional at Royal Troon in the summer of 1997.

Confused? Here's a quick resume.

When Woods turned professional in August 1996, it was with the record of having won the last three US Amateurs and the reputation of being almost invincible. Things would obviously change once he joined the big boys as a pro, and indeed they did. But not by much.

In the two months of the USPGA Tour season remaining to him, he niftily secured his player's card by winning two tournaments. The first week of 1997, he won the season-opening Mercedes Championship by almost holing his tee shot on the first play-off hole to beat Tom Lehman, the reigning Open champion.

In February 1997, he won the Asian Honda Classic in Thailand by 10 shots. As you might expect, critics cavilled that he could only do that because the field was weak. Two months later, he went to Augusta and won the Masters by 12. No one was making the same complaint twice.

He was now perhaps the most sought-after celebrity in the world — as someone (in fact, myself) put it, he could probably have got a date with Lara Croft had he wanted.

By the time he arrived at Royal Troon, Tiger had also won the GTE Byron Nelson Classic and the Motorola Western Open. He had been thwarted by the tight fairways and heavy rough at the US Open, but he was well fancied to be able to cope with a links and notch up his second victory in a major championship.

In fact, it took him two days to get acclimatised, but his 64 on Saturday was a masterpiece, including two unforgettable cameos of genius in the form of an eagle on the 16th and a chip-in birdie at the 17th. That got him into contention, but on Sunday afternoon his putter took him out of it by missing short birdie putts on the sixth and seventh before the 'Postage Stamp' franked him for a triple-bogey 6.

Since — although by no means necessarily because of — that chastening experience, Woods had won just twice between leaving Britain and returning to it. In Thailand (again) in January, he had brilliantly overhauled a faltering Ernie Els with a closing 65 and then ensnared him in a play-off. In May, he took his first USPGA Tour title for over 10 months by winning the BellSouth Classic in Atlanta.

With six other top-10 USPGA Tour finishes, Tiger's golf in 1998 had been far from mediocre by anybody's standards. But then Tiger is no more an anybody than … well, than Lara Croft's body. His standards aren't so much high as stratospheric. He has not merely been encumbered by great expectations but burdened as a deliverer of sporting miracles; his story not so much Dickensian as neo-Biblical. Given all of that, to lead this year's Open after the first day was a pretty impressive performance.

To be strictly accurate, it has to be conceded that Woods did not hold the lead alone. He shared it with fellow American John Huston. However, this in itself could have been interpreted as a happy harbinger. When Woods won the 1997 Masters, Huston had been the first-round leader. (No one apart from

After the first round, Woods didn't putt well.

Tiger got much of a look-in after that.)

Tiger's bid for the 1998 Open got underway at 9.55 on a gently pleasant Thursday morning, the threat of rain receding all the while, in the company of Nick Price and Per-Ulrik Johansson. Woods had spent the week before playing some of the marvellous links of Ireland in the company of his good friend and successor as Masters champion, Mark O'Meara.

Those experiences may have encouraged him to realise that with his awesome length, he need only go with his driver on four holes at Royal Birkdale. His first birdie of the day landed at the third, where a five iron off the tee was followed by a pitching wedge to 10 feet. That birdie putt disappeared, as did others from 12 feet at the fifth and from 20 feet at the seventh.

The 411-yard ninth was one of the holes where he decided on the driver. He used it, wind-assisted, to knock the ball to within 50 feet of the stick. A pitch and a six-foot putt later, and he had reached the turn in 30, four under par.

"To me, it makes no sense to lay up," he would say of the ninth afterwards. "I can carry that bunker and put it right on the green. There is no rough down there. I didn't really kill it. I hit a normal drive, got it up in the wind, and it carried." Put another way, a shot that most of us regarded as both risky and thrilling was sensible and mundane.

Into the second nine, Woods suffered his first reverse at the short 12th, where he over-shot the green with a six iron and missed a three-foot putt for par. A birdie from 30 feet helped compensate for that just one hole later, and both of Birkdale's two par-5s yielded birdies.

At the 15th, a fine drive was capped by a majestic two iron, which set up a fairly simple chip-and-putt 4. The 17th, playing in the opposite direction, was a three wood, six iron, two-putt type of birdie for Tiger. Unfortunately, the round ended somewhat sourly when he hit an eight iron over the green on the 18th and missed from eight feet for the par 4 that would have earned him the outright lead.

The 65 not only matched Huston's effort of some 80 minutes previously, it put Woods in the clubhouse a stroke ahead of playing partner Price. He was asked what Tiger had done best. "Manage his game," he replied.

Price then went on to amplify that remark in the invariably thoughtful fashion that Nick does. "It looked like he throttled back a little today, which is good to see. He went hard at one shot, which was a two iron into 15, where he went pretty flat out. He had 241 yards and he hit a two iron six or seven yards past the pin. (Squeamish readers might prefer not to know that Birkdale's 15th measures 544 yards and was playing pretty well directly into the wind.) That's the only one I saw him go hard at. A year ago, he used to do that a little more frequently."

Price, a winner himself of three majors, including the 1994 Open, continued, "He'll mature. He's learning every year. I think he is diligent enough to go out there and refine and round off the rough edges. He's got so much talent. I think he can, just as Jack Nicklaus and all the great players before him have done, get better and better with age."

And, with a twinkle, Price said, "If he continues to get better and better, by the time he gets to 30, he's going to be a pretty good player."

So there's hope for him yet, then.

Price's interview ended with the press officer declaring, "Gentlemen, sorry to cut it short. We have someone else waiting."

Guess who?

The man himself was largely graciousness personified, "The ovation I got at 18, I haven't had that in a long time and it felt really good." The Tiger of a year ago — to be honest, most professionals of today — would have had the recollection ruined by the memory of that recent bogey.

Woods was similarly generous about Royal Birkdale, saying, "I love this golf course because it is extremely difficult but it is fair. All the trouble is right in front of you. It makes it very enjoyable because it's like you get these lanes you have to hit through. You stray from those lanes, you're going to get penalised, and that's how it should be."

And he delivered a paean to links golf. "I love it over here. I would rather play this type of golf than our stadium golf back home. You have more options," he said. "You have to be very creative in order to play over here. I think that is why Seve has done so well. You have to see these shots and these lies and get a feel in your hands."

It was at Royal Birkdale in the 1976 Open that Severiano Ballesteros first burst into prominence, finishing runner-up as a 19-year-old. Tiger was then barely six months old. Seve would win the Open within three years. After the first round in 1998, Woods had reason to hope the delay might only be three days.

In fact, it will be longer than that. Having last year usurped Ballesteros as the youngest Masters winner in history, Woods can no longer deprive him of the honour of being the youngest winner of the Open this century. But that does not mean he won't ever be crowned as champion. As his close friend, Orlando neighbour and successor as holder of the Masters title, Mark O'Meara, later put it during the course of his own celebrations on the Sunday evening, "I imagine his name will be on this trophy some day, too."

"I made a whole bunch of mistakes this week," Woods admitted when this one was over. There weren't so many in his second round of 73, but his 77 on Saturday, shot (for the third day running) in the company of Price, did prove calamitous. It seemed that on every hole, Tiger would stand over a five- or six-foot putt, either for a par or a birdie (more commonly the latter), and every time, it seemed, he would miss it. On every occasion, one was reminded not so much of how he didn't miss from inside 10 feet during the entire 72 holes of the 1997 Masters as of the fact that he ranked 126th in putting on the USPGA Tour coming into the Open.

The resultant third-round 77 left Woods at five over par for the championship, and five shots off the pace. After what he had just been through, it would require a super-human effort to get back into contention, but then Tiger spent most of his first 12 months as a professional rendering the magnificent as the mundane. Super-human was duly close to what we got, even if he began in the manner of the day before, three-putting the first green from 18 feet.

In fact, he never genuinely threatened to win the championship until the 15th hole. Four over par playing this par-5, Woods got a terrific break when he carved his drive to the right — so far right that he found an untypically good lie in the rough. Typically, he exploited the break to hammer a three wood onto the fringe of the green. Equally characteristically, when the 30-foot chip went close enough to clinch the birdie, he wasn't delighted but annoyed. The eagle had not landed.

After a par at the 16th, the 17th — an easier par-5 than the 15th — seemed to have thwarted him when he took three shots to get to the green. To be accurate, they got him over it, some 40 feet from the cup. Woods, being Tiger, had the solution. The chip went down for another birdie.

Two over par with one hole to play, he was two shots off the pace. He needed a birdie at the last. Two fine iron shots later, he faced a 30-foot putt for it. You just knew it was going to go in. And it did.

Within moments, O'Meara had bogeyed the 16th. At that moment, indeed for several more, Woods had a share of the lead of the Open. But, of course, he had finished. The destiny of the title now lay exclusively in the hands of others. And one of them took full advantage.

Justin Rose (138) shot 66 to equal the amateur record of Frank Stranahan in 1950 and Tiger Woods in 1996.

AN AMATEUR SHOWS THE WAY

BY ROBERT SOMMERS

Links courses need foul weather to protect them from the modern professional golfer, who can drive the ball nearly 300 yards and play a five iron more than 200. Royal Birkdale is stronger than most, but the sunshine and light winds of the first round showed how vulnerable it can be in pleasant weather.

While Thursday's round had been played under mild conditions, Friday's began in rain and ended in strong winds that not only tested the shotmaking of the entire field, but turned Royal Birkdale into a mean test of shotmaking and grit as well.

A light drizzle began about 7 o'clock, 15 minutes before the first group teed off, but by 7.30 rain gushed down in sheets, slacked off for a while, then struck hard again at about 10.30. It finally eased off around noon; the clouds broke up, the sun shined through, and the wind freshened, blowing steadily at around 25 miles an hour and gusting above 30.

After the heavy mid-morning downpour, someone raised the question of whether the course was playable. Hugh Campbell, Chairman of the Royal and Ancient Golf Club's Championship Committee, said he hadn't even considered suspending play, but he added that although the greens were shedding water, puddles had built up on some tees. The course was still playable, so the championship kept on schedule.

Then, in late afternoon, Campbell did suspend play. He said that lightning had been reported over the Irish Sea, within sight of Royal Birkdale's high dunes, and then a wind calculated at 50 miles an hour swept in from the sea, buffeting the golfers, bending the flagsticks, and moving golf balls at rest on the greens. Play was suspended at 5.27 and resumed at 6.05, when the storm passed and the weather improved.

Where crowds had flocked into Birkdale before the first starting time on Thursday, the early Friday starters played before only a scattered few spectators, if any at all. It was a damp, cold, miserable day. The scoring showed it.

Where 27 men had shot in the 60s in the opening round, only seven scored under 70 in the second, and seven others matched par. Where the field averaged 72.1 in the first round, it averaged 74.8 in the second, nearly three strokes higher.

Some of the scores were disheartening. After opening with 65, John Huston lost his magnetism and shot 77; Tiger Woods, who had matched Huston's 65, slipped to 73; Loren Roberts went from 66 to 76, Fred Couples from 66 to 74, Nick Price from 66 to 72, Davis Love III from 67 to 73, and Vijay Singh from 67 to 74.

The leading European players remained conspicuously out of the leading positions, with only Thomas Bjorn, of Denmark, and Jesper Parnevik, of Sweden, amongst the 11 players at level par or better. There were still six Americans in that group. Fredrik Jacobson, of Sweden, went from 67 to 78 and European Order of Merit leader Lee Westwood, from England, was tied for 22nd place at 142.

On a day made for holding on to what you had, others gained ground. Brian Watts shot 69 and moved into first place, at 137, three under par; Mark O'Meara shot 68 and moved into a tie for sixth place at 140, and Lee Janzen, Tom Kite, Scott Dunlap and Des Smyth climbed in the standings by shooting 69s.

Extraordinary though those rounds may have been under the circumstances, all the professionals were out-played by Justin Rose, a 17-year-old English amateur, from Hampshire. Rose shot 66, two strokes better than O'Meara, whose 68 was the best of the professionals.

With his astounding score, Rose shot into a tie for second place with Woods and Price at 138, one stroke behind Watts. Thomas Bjorn followed his opening 68 with 71 and still climbed from a tie for 11th into fifth place, at 139, followed by Love,

Brian Watts (137), with scores of 68 and 69, demonstrated the ability that had earned 11 victories in Japan.

Tiger Woods (138) struggled with five bogeys before finishing with 73 on two birdies.

O'Meara, Couples, Stephen Ames, Jim Furyk, and Jesper Parnevik, at 140, level par.

Rose was a prodigy. In August of 1997 he had become the third 17-year-old to play for the Walker Cup, an amateur team match between Great Britain and Ireland on the one side and the United States on the other. The youngest of the three, Rose won two points for his side.

While it is always surprising for one so young to play so extraordinarily well on such an important occasion, Rose had given signs he was no ordinary young golfer three years earlier. At 14, he had nearly qualified for the 1995 Open.

As a Walker Cup player, he was exempt from the first stage of qualifying for the 1998 Open and made it into the starting field in the second stage by placing second among 13 qualifiers at the Hillside Golf Club, which abuts Birkdale. He made the most of the opportunity.

Tall and lean, befitting one so young, Rose had been called by David Leadbetter one of the finest 17-year-old golfers he had seen. "He has oodles of talent," Leadbetter said.

Leadbetter had looked over Justin's swing in Orlando, Florida, and made only a few suggestions. After the ease with which Rose handled Royal Birkdale, no one else dared offer advice.

Truthfully, though, Rose had done little else than play golf for some time. He had left school at the age of 16 and had played steadily for the last year and a half.

Admittedly Rose had the best of Birkdale's weather. He began at 11.30, just as the clouds were breaking up and before the wind reached its full force. Even with the improving weather, his round didn't look promising at the start. He three-putted the third from six feet, but he played the remaining 15 holes in five under par, despite making two more bogeys.

Justin began his assault by holing birdie putts of 20 feet on the fourth and six feet on the fifth, after a neat nine iron. He lost another stroke at the difficult sixth, where his two-iron approach drifted into heavy grass, but he struck back by playing the ninth with a four iron and six iron and holing a mammoth putt of perhaps 50 feet.

Out in 33, one under par, Rose cruised through the next four holes in level par, then struck again, drilling a three iron onto the 14th green, the par-3, and running in his putt from 25 feet. Rose was two under par now, but he gave away a stroke on the 16th by

Nick Price (138) took his second of four bogeys here at the ninth from a plugged lie, but made eagle on the 17th for 72.

bunkering his two-iron approach and missing from five feet.

Rose was still one under par with two holes to play. Once again the wind was at his back on the 17th. Thinking clearly, Rose put aside his driver and teed off with a three wood. The ball flew so far down the middle of the narrow fairway he had only a seven iron left. He hit it within 10 feet of the hole and eagled.

Three under par now, Rose had only the 472-yard 18th to play. It, too, played with the wind. Rose drove with a two iron, lofted an eight iron to 20 feet, and, of course, holed the putt. He had come back in 33 and had matched the lowest score an amateur had ever shot in the Open. The American Frank Stranahan had shot 66 at Troon in 1950, and Tiger Woods had matched it at Royal Lytham and St Annes in 1996.

Rose wasn't the only mystery in this Open. When Brian Watts rushed to the top, hardly anyone had heard of him. It turned out he was 32 years old and had been born in Canada to an English father and

German mother who emigrated to Texas, where Brian grew up. After going off to Oklahoma State University, he won the 1987 National Collegiate Athletic Association (NCAA) Championship, the biggest college tournament in the United States, then turned to professional golf.

He had a fling on the USPGA Tour but lost his player's card, and had spent five years playing in Japan. He had done very well. He had not only won 11 tournaments since 1994, he had not finished outside the leading 10 in the Japanese Order of Merit. Furthermore, he had climbed to 35th place in the World Ranking, ahead of Nick Faldo, Tom Kite and Ian Woosnam.

Coming into the Open, Watts ranked sixth on the Japanese Order of Merit with winnings of ¥43,512,580, roughly £210,000, not a bad living, even if the living was out of a suitcase.

Expounding on his career in Japan, Watts said, "The competition is a bit less intense there than in the United States, where the standard is high, right down to the last player in every tournament. But the

Davis Love III (140) said, "If you lose your patience you make a bad score, and I did that a couple of times."

Stephen Ames (140) said his "swing felt good considering the conditions."

Fred Couples (140) didn't birdie either par-5.

Jim Furyk (140) had two rounds of 70.

Mark O'Meara (140) shot 68, one of just seven below-par rounds.

Japan Tour is the third best in the world, and I'm lucky to be able to play there."

Still, he dreamt of returning to the American Tour, saying, "Perhaps I might do well in enough foreign tournaments they'll count toward my tour card."

He seemed to have the game. He swung with a legato tempo and never rushed a shot, even in the tensest circumstances. He appeared sound emotionally as well. Certainly he held up to the gripping pressure of the Open.

This had been Watts' sixth Open. So far he had never placed higher than a tie for 40th at St Andrews in 1995, and he had missed the cut in the last two Opens.

Teeing off at 8.25 in the midst of the rain, Watts had a tough start. He drove into the right rough and bogeyed the first, but he picked up two quick birdies on the second and third with first-class pitches to 15 feet and 10 feet. Quickly, though, he lost both strokes. His four-iron tee shot to the par-3 fourth drifted into heavy grass; he hacked it to the collar, and three-putted. Two holes later he drove into the left rough of the devilish sixth, took two more to reach the green, and two-putted from 25 feet.

By then the sky had cleared and the wind was just beginning to rise. From then on, Watts played nearly

Thomas Bjorn (139) was alone in fifth place.

Jesper Parnevik (140) struggled with his putting.

Gordon Brand Jnr (141) was pleased with his start.

flawless golf. He picked up one birdie on the seventh by holing from 30 feet, another on the 12th with a stunning four iron to five feet, and his final birdie on the 17th, where he reached the green with a four-iron second and two-putted. Back in 34, Watts had taken command of the championship, an unexpected role.

Asked about the conditions he played under, Watts said, "You want to enjoy them, but I don't want to lie to you. It's really tough out there. I can't say I enjoyed playing in it, but I deal with it as it comes."

Watts had finished just ahead of O'Meara, who made a giant move himself, climbing from a tie for 62nd place into a contending position. He did it by shooting the second lowest round of the day, and considering that he played under wretched conditions, his was a good score indeed. He had warmed up in the rain and played the first five or six holes not only over soggy ground but with the wind coming from a different direction. It not only shifted when he reached the second tee, but it picked up strength as well, driving the rain horizontally. Soon, though, the weather eased and the rain slowed and finally quit.

O'Meara claimed he had played much better than he had in the first round. "I drove a bit better," he said, "and I kept the ball in play. I hit a lot of fairways and a lot of greens. I didn't knock down the flags, but I had a lot of chances."

O'Meara said he hit many of those greens with four irons, which he called the day's club of choice. He used it first on the second with a superb shot to three feet and again on the 12th, with another to six feet. He birdied them both, but reached the 17th tee at level par because of bogeys on the third, where he missed the green with a nine iron, and the 16th, where he pulled his drive into the left rough, his worst tee shot of the day.

With the wind at his back, he struck a good drive on the 17th, then lofted a seven iron into the wind. It hit the green and rolled within 15 feet of the cup, set in the right front corner. The putt fell for an eagle 3 and he had his 68.

Woods, meantime, saved a mediocre round by birdieing the two finishing holes. He had gone out in 38 and dropped another stroke at the 15th, a par-5, where two shots — his drive and his third — fell into bunkers. Five over par then, he played a three wood into the 17th fairway and a seven iron into another bunker. A pitch to six feet and he had one birdie, then a pitching wedge to 12 feet on the last for another birdie.

Woods had been caught in the worst of the weather. One of the late starters, going off at 2.25 in the afternoon, he was on the 11th hole when the high winds roared in from the sea and, he said, moved his ball on the green, which led to the suspension of play. His putting had been erratic. He three-putted the second from 15 feet, missed from eight feet on the sixth and from 10 feet on the ninth.

Still, Tiger remained in the thick of the battle and said he had come out of a difficult round, "smelling like a rose."

Huston didn't. Spraying shots from one side of the fairway to the other, he went out in 37, with a double-bogey 6 on the fifth, and stumbled home in 40. His 142 left him safely in the field for the final two rounds, but he would play no further part in deciding the championship.

Tom Kite (141), a Texan, was used to the wind.

Lee Janzen (141) shot 69 in the second round.

Peter Baker (141) shot 72 with two birdies and four bogeys.

Raymond Russell (141) stayed close to the lead.

Nor would Justin Leonard, who had so charmed the galleries when he won at Royal Troon the previous year, not only with his demeanour but with his sensational golf as well. Leonard simply didn't play well. Assuming he had missed the cut when he put up his second 73, he thought he would fly to Dallas, then decided to wait. The cut fell at 146, and he was in.

Neither of his two immediate predecessors as Open champions made it, though. John Daly had another of his periodic flights from reason, made 10 on the 18th hole by taking seven strokes from bunkers, shot 78 and 151.

Tom Lehman, the 1996 champion, shot 79 and 150, but he had an excuse. Playing with his children, he had toppled over and hurt himself in the fall. He admitted he felt stiff and sore.

Then there was Colin Montgomerie, who tried so hard and yet failed once again, the fifth time in nine Open starts that he had missed the cut. He fought on to the end, finishing with an eagle 3 on the 17th and a birdie 3 on the 18th, but the damage had been done. He simply could not hole a putt and three-putted four greens. Montgomerie shot 74 and 147, one stroke too many.

Other well-established players were eliminated as well. With 149, Tom Watson, who had come to

Royal Birkdale with so much confidence, missed by three strokes, only his fourth missed cut in 23 starts in the Open. He was among five men missing the cut who among them had won 13 Opens. Watson had won five, Severiano Ballesteros had won three, Daly and Lehman one apiece, and the ageless Gary Player had won his first in 1959, fully 39 years earlier, his second in 1968 and his third in 1974. Player shot 151.

The cut also caught Jeff Maggert, Bob Tway, Bernhard Langer, Paul Azinger, Frank Nobilo, Ben Crenshaw and the American amateur Matt Kuchar, who had been low amateur in both the Masters and the US Open. Kuchar shot two rounds of 75 and was last amongst the five amateurs in the field.

It had been a trying round, indeed. Worse was coming.

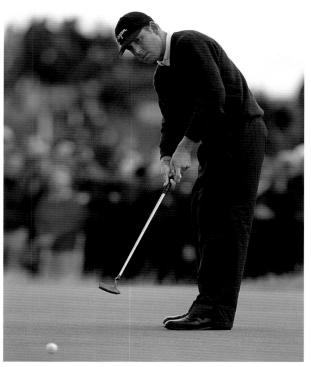

Justin Leonard (146) finished on the cut score.

Jose Maria Olazabal (145) survived the cut.

Sergio Garcia (144) was among three amateurs left.

SECOND ROUND RESULTS

HOLE	1	2	3	4	5	6	7	8	9	10	11	12	13	14	15	16	17	18	
PAR	4	4	4	3	4	4	3	4	4	4	4	3	4	3	5	4	5	4	TOTAL
Brian Watts	5	3	3	5	4	5	2	4	4	4	4	2	4	3	5	4	4	4	69-137
*Justin Rose	4	4	5	2	3	5	3	4	3	4	4	3	4	2	5	5	3	3	66-138
Tiger Woods	5	5	4	3	4	5	3	4	5	4	4	3	4	3	6	4	4	3	73-138
Nick Price	4	4	4	3	4	5	3	4	5	5	4	3	4	3	5	5	3	4	72-138
Thomas Bjorn	5	4	3	3	4	4	3	4	4	4	5	3	5	3	5	4	4	4	71-139
Davis Love III	4	3	5	3	5	4	3	4	4	4	6	3	4	3	5	5	4	4	73-140
Mark O'Meara	4	3	5	3	4	4	3	4	4	4	4	2	4	3	5	5	3	4	68-140
Fred Couples	5	4	4	3	4	5	3	5	5	4	4	3	5	3	5	4	5	3	74-140
Stephen Ames	4	5	4	4	5	3	4	4	4	5	4	3	4	6	4	3	3		72-140
Jim Furyk	4	4	3	4	3	5	3	4	4	4	4	3	4	4	5	4	4	4	70-140
Jesper Parnevik	3	4	5	3	4	5	3	4	5	4	4	3	3	4	5	4	5	4	72-140
Gordon Brand Jnr	4	4	3	3	4	5	3	5	4	4	4	3	3	3	4	4	5	5	70-141
David Duval	4	4	4	4	4	4	3	4	4	4	4	3	4	3	4	5	4	5	71-141
Vijay Singh	5	5	3	3	5	4	4	4	4	3	4	4	4	4	5	5	4	4	74-141
Raymond Russell	4	5	4	4	4	4	3	4	4	4	4	3	5	3	5	5	4	4	73-141
Lee Janzen	6	4	4	3	4	4	4	4	3	4	4	3	4	2	5	4	4	4	69-141
Tom Kite	5	3	4	3	4	4	3	4	4	4	3	3	5	3	5	4	5	3	69-141
Scott Dunlap	4	5	4	3	3	4	4	3	4	4	4	4	4	2	5	4	4	4	69-141
Peter Baker	4	4	4	3	3	5	3	4	5	4	5	3	4	4	5	4	4	4	72-141
Brad Faxon	5	4	4	4	3	5	3	4	4	5	5	2	4	4	5	5	4	4	74-141
Eduardo Romero	4	4	4	3	4	6	3	3	3	4	4	3	4	4	5	4	4	4	70-141

* Denotes amateur

HOLE SUMMARY

HOLE	PAR	EAGLES	BIRDIES	PARS	BOGEYS	HIGHER	RANK	AVERAGE
1	4	0	8	70	67	9	3	4.52
2	4	0	15	84	49	6	6	4.31
3	4	0	20	119	15	0	17	3.97
4	3	0	9	101	41	3	11	3.25
5	4	0	15	98	36	5	15	4.20
6	4	0	1	55	78	20	1	4.79
7	3	0	11	93	47	3	9	3.27
8	4	0	7	108	34	5	11	4.25
9	4	0	7	86	59	2	5	4.36
OUT	34	0	93	814	426	53		36.91
10	4	0	15	86	46	7	6	4.31
11	4	0	5	85	52	12	4	4.49
12	3	0	6	109	37	2	13	3.23
13	4	0	12	105	35	2	16	4.18
14	3	0	12	99	41	2	14	3.23
15	5	1	15	92	37	9	10	5.25
16	4	0	5	74	63	12	2	4.54
17	5	18	77	47	10	2	18	4.36
18	4	0	14	93	40	7	8	4.29
IN	36	19	161	790	361	55		37.87
TOTAL	70	19	254	1604	787	108		74.78

Players Below Par	7
Players At Par	7
Players Above Par	140

LOW SCORES

Low First Nine	*Justin Rose	33
Low Second Nine	Santiago Luna	33
	*Justin Rose	33
Low Round	*Justin Rose	66

WEATHER

Temperature: low 12°C, high 20°C.
9.4mm rain, strong southwest winds.

Justin Rose said, "I was thinking clearly and hitting the shots I wanted to hit, and holing the putts at the end."

COMMENTARY

ROSE HAS A WEEK OF DREAMS

BY ANDREW FARRELL

If anything was certain about the 127th Open Championship, the course and conditions facing the 156 competitors, it was going to sort out the men from the boys. What no one was expecting was that a Boy Wonder would come along to show everyone else how to do it.

That's why it is called "The Open." The world's oldest golf championship is open to anyone who is good enough. For Justin Rose, two weeks short of his 18th birthday, it was a dream just to be playing at Royal Birkdale. As for many others playing in their first Open, that experience may have remained to be shared mainly with family and friends had not Rose stepped out of his private dreamland and into the very public land of fairy tales on a wet, windy Friday afternoon by the seaside.

This does not happen at regular tournaments, the ones that combine to form the treadmills that are the professional tours around the globe. Majors championships are different. Here was a 17-year-old amateur upstaging the finest professionals in the world. When Rose contrived to finish his second round with an eagle at the 17th and a birdie at the last, his 66 was two strokes better than the best of the rest, who just happened to be the reigning Masters champion and the eventual Open champion, Mark O'Meara.

Rose received a mighty ovation, despite the grandstands around the 18th green not being as full as they would be on Sunday evening. The sound is worth storing in the memory to use as a comparison with the thunderous eruption that greeted Rose as he completed the 72nd hole two days later, but at the time there was no knowing how long this fairy tale would last, or to what flight of fancy it might ascend.

Just for the minute, the facts were these. The course was thought to offer a demanding test of golf in calm conditions, but combined with the gales was described as "brutal." Yet Rose's four-under-par round

was just one stroke more than Tiger Woods and John Huston had scored the previous day in ideal conditions. It was seven better than Woods on the day and 11 better than Huston, and tied the record low round for an amateur, set by Frank Stranahan in 1950 and tied by Woods at Royal Lytham in 1996. After 36 holes, Rose was one stroke behind the leader, Brian Watts, and level with Woods and Nick Price at two under par.

"That's one of my best rounds and to play it in these circumstances is fantastic," Rose told the media afterwards. One of the best? "Well, actually, the best round probably." Had he ever imagined his name on the leaderboard at the Open? "At the end of the Open at Troon last year they had a sign up there: 'Well done, Justin' and that's something that stayed in my mind ever since."

Rose added, "I guess I wasn't worried about the conditions. My caddie and I were choosing the right shots, I was thinking clearly and, you know, luckily hitting the shots I wanted to hit and then holing the putts at the end." Who were his role models? "I love Ernie Els' swing and Nick Price is a role model for me. He's got a great fighting spirit on the course, and off the course he is a gentleman. He gives everybody time."

This sort of thing may have been new to Rose, although you would not have known, but not to the media. The year of 1998 had been full of amateur sensations. At the Masters, Matt Kuchar, the US Amateur champion, first showed his smile to the world when finishing 21st. At the US Open, Kuchar, 20, did it again, sharing 14th place and in the process gaining exemptions for next year for both the first two majors. Europe's answer to Kuchar seemed to be Sergio Garcia, the 18-year-old Spaniard who became the 1997 Catalan PGA champion before taking the 1998 British Amateur at Muirfield.

Rose tied the record for an amateur with 66 in the second round after this 10-foot putt for eagle 3 at the 17th.

Unlike Kuchar and Garcia, Rose had to qualify for the Open and had thrown off his bout of flu by the time he teed up at Hillside on the Sunday prior to the Open. He scored 74 in the first round and dropped shots on the first nine the following day. After a double bogey at the second hole, he turned to the golf writer from his local paper in Hook, Hampshire, and said, "Don't worry." Four under par on the back nine gave Rose a 72 and left him only a shot behind the leading qualifier at Hillside, Thomas Levet.

Now there was a scramble for accommodation in Southport for Rose, his father Ken and mother Annie and sister Margi. Brother Brandon, a former player on the South African Tour, turned up briefly but flew back to South Africa.

The family had left Johannesburg when Rose was five years of age. By then Rose already had his first set of proper clubs. At 11 months, he had received a plastic ball and club. "He became besotted with it," his father said. "He became so proficient he could hit the ball 30 yards." Justin became a cabaret act at his parents' dinner parties. "I was determined to introduce him to golf at the earliest stage. Golf seems to have a code of ethics for life itself."

Rose became a prolific winner at junior level and won the St Andrews Links Trophy when he was 16 in 1997. Later that season, just after his 17th birthday, Rose became the youngest player to appear in the Walker Cup. Although he hit the first ball at Quaker Ridge out of bounds, he was the star of the Great Britain and Ireland team.

He could have been in the England team at the age of 14 and it was at that age, in 1995, that Rose became the youngest to play in Final Qualifying for the Open.

It was there that the tradition started of his parents wearing roses in their hats. Ken Rose was his son's teacher. "We couldn't afford a full-time coach, so I taught him the fundamentals and that meant a very simple, basic swing. What I didn't know was what a dynamic package I had in terms of talent." Rose left school at 16 with eight GCSEs. "College is something I would have liked to have done but golf at that point was more important and still is."

Rose's height brought worries about his swing, much the same as Nick Faldo has always had, and so an approach was made to Faldo's coach, David Leadbetter. Rose spent a week in Orlando, Florida, in March and Leadbetter was impressed enough to leave his swing pretty much alone. "There is no question he is one of the best 17-year-olds I have ever seen," Leadbetter said. Ken Rose added, "He may look like a gangly kid but he is incredibly strong. Just look at his hands. They are capable of strangling a tiger."

That's what the British press reported he had done on Saturday morning. Rose looked at few of the photos — How could he miss them on the front pages? — and left the newspapers for his family to read. He went up to the course in the morning to do some chipping, but had a long wait until his 3.10 starting time. By now, Kuchar had missed the cut and Garcia played his weekend golf early in the mornings. More than that, Colin Montgomerie, Europe's five-time No. 1, had made an early departure, while Faldo and Lee Westwood, Britain's last golfing superstar and his heir apparent, never troubled the leaderboard operators.

This was the worst day yet. In the match in front, Woods struggled to 77 and Price slumped dramatically to 82. Rose bogeyed the first two holes. So he wasn't superhuman after all. Nerves could get the better of him. But the encouragement of the gallery kept him going. He did not drop another shot on the first nine and briefly tied for the lead with Watts. "That was a great feeling," said Rose, whose 75 left him two shots off the lead with 18 holes to play.

"I wasn't uncomfortable with that situation. I had started bogey, bogey and you're thinking, 'Well, this is a dubious start.' Then I made a few pars and I began to feel I was getting the better of the course. I didn't have a great finish but I'm very happy. Starting the day, I didn't realise it would be anything like that. Walking up every hole I got an ovation, a bit like Jack Nicklaus. It was incredible. People were shouting my name and that pushed me on."

And so thoughts turned to the next day. Could he become the first amateur to win the Open since Bobby Jones took the third of his three titles in 1930? Would having to turn down the £300,000 first prize be like winning the lottery but losing the ticket? "It would be such a great achievement to win the claret jug you wouldn't be thinking of the money," he responded. "To tell you the truth I'm not sure what the prize money is. It would take my best

round ever to win, a monumental effort, so I'm not predicting anything."

If he did, his questioners persisted, what would he do next? "I guess when I'm 18 then you have got to win the Masters, and then 19 win the US Open, and 20 win the USPGA."

A bogey at the first hole on Sunday meant Rose was never quite close enough to challenge for the lead. Watts and O'Meara were doing that. But Rose never disappeared, either, even after going to the turn in two over. He came home in three under. He holed from 12 feet at the 12th, then two-putted for a birdie at the 15th after hitting a drive and a three wood onto the green, and then he came to the last.

His drive was wildly hooked, over the barrier holding back the gallery. In order to clear the barrier, he could not hit more than a five iron and came up short in the left-hand rough. He had 38 yards to carry the greenside bunker and 45 yards to the hole. Twelve years earlier, Severiano Ballesteros, 19 and new to the world, played an audacious chip-and-run from off the 18th green at Birkdale and, though Johnny Miller won the title then, Seve stole the hearts and minds of the those who were watching.

Now Rose did something similar, with one exception. He holed the shot. The cacophony of sound was fit for an Open champion itself. The roars just got louder and louder. "I can't believe it," Rose said trying to describe the moment. "I mean, it was a tough shot out of the rough, over a bunker. I said to my caddie, 'I'm going for the shot, try to get it close.' I could have bailed out but I had nothing to lose. It was one of those incredible moments — the ball got nearer and nearer the hole and finally disappeared. I couldn't believe it.

"The whole week has been really, really special for me and to finish on that note was in context with the whole week. At the beginning of my week I just wanted to be a part of it. I didn't realise I would be such a part of it. I almost felt like the winner coming up the 18th hole. I was put at ease by the crowd. The incredible support I had didn't give me time to be nervous. I went out there, had a lot of fun and luckily played well."

Brian Watts (210) salvaged a 73 to lead by two strokes after being five over par through 12 holes.

WATTS HOLDS AGAINST THE WIND

BY ROBERT SOMMERS

Five players entered the third round under par, but at the end of a brutal day, not one had held his position. Instead, only Brian Watts held at level-par 210 for the 54 holes, while Jesper Parnevik, Jim Furyk and Mark O'Meara stood two strokes behind, at 212.

Playing that well was not a simple accomplishment. The wonder is they scored so low. The day was cold and overcast, and winds stronger than those of the second round battered the players and turned a round at Royal Birkdale into torture. Balls couldn't be controlled, and some holes simply couldn't be played. The sixth, which again played directly into the wind, could be reached only with two drivers, and the first and second were as tough as any. The first gave up only two birdies and the second just one. No one birdied the sixth or the 11th, a simple par-4 of 408 yards.

Of the 24 leaders after 54 holes, only 10 parred the first, at 449 yards a vicious starting hole, and only 13 parred the second, which some consider tougher. More than one player couldn't drive the ball far enough to reach the fairway.

O'Meara, Fred Couples and Lee Janzen made 6s on the first, Janzen followed with another on the second, and Peter Baker made 7 on the second after bogeying the first. Those two holes ruined Lee Westwood. The winner at Loch Lomond the previous week, Westwood had shot two rounds of 71, but he started the third round with a 6 on the first, a 7 on the second, and a 5 on the third — six strokes gone in three holes. With 78 he fell like a rock.

Flags flying above the grandstands snapped in the gale-like winds as the field averaged 77.5 strokes. Of the 81 men who started, 23 shot in the 80s and only 13 shot under 75. The course embarrassed some great players. Lee Janzen shot 80, Justin Leonard and Nick Price both shot 82s, and Phil Mickelson shot 85. Both Price and Mickelson played the second nine in 45. Mickelson played the last seven holes in nine over par, and Price had 10 5s, five 4s and one 6.

That Costantino Rocca and Katsuyoshi Tomori shot par 70s approached wizardry, and that young Justin Rose held his composure in such winds prompted suspicions of sorcery. By playing such a phenomenal round, Rose earned the applause he was given when he strode down the final fairway all aglow.

Through all the carnage only one voice rose in protest, and even that complaint was mild. Ian Woosnam suggested that the R and A might have moved the tee markers forward on some holes. Everyone else seemed to agree there wasn't much the R and A could have done to ease the conditions, which truly prevented the players from playing the shots they not only had to play but could have played in calmer weather. The winds simply took away their skills. Controlling a ball in the wind is a fine art, but it was futile this day.

As the results began coming in, Sir Michael Bonallack, Secretary of the R and A, addressed what he looked on as a frustrating dilemma. "We cut the greens only once instead of twice so they would not be too quick," he said, "but, really, there is a limit to what we could do. It is a shame. The wind is just too strong for it to be a fair test."

Among the 36-hole leaders, Woods shot 77 and dropped from a tie for second into a tie for sixth; Price, with his 82, fell from a tie for second to a tie for 30th, and Couples plunged 10 places, from a tie for sixth to a tie for 16th. Even though he shot 76, Thomas Bjorn dropped only one place, from fifth to a tie for sixth.

Others, though, gained ground with rounds that would have cost them on any other day. Furyk, Parnevik and O'Meara moved up with 72s, climbing

Tied for second in 1997, Jesper Parnevik (212) shot 72 and was "very pleased to have another chance to win it."

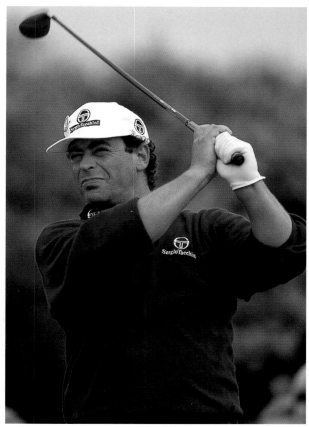

Japan's Katsuyoshi Tomori (left) and Italy's Costantino Rocca (right) shot level-par 70s. Both were on 216.

into a tie for second, and John Huston re-appeared, making up for his second-round 77 by shooting 73 and climbing from a tie for 22nd into a tie for sixth.

Tomori and Rocca gained the most of anyone. Barely making the cut with their 146s, they jumped past 52 players, from a tie for 65th to a tie for 10th with David Duval and the Scot Raymond Russell.

Both men played exceptionally steady golf. A native of Okinawa, a Japanese-owned island about 350 miles south of the home islands, Tomori played Royal Birkdale with three birdies and three bogeys. With four holes to play he stood one under par, but he three-putted the 15th and bunkered his approach to the 16th. One over par now, he drove with a three wood on the 17th and reached the green with a seven iron. Two putts and he was back to level par.

Asked if the wind on the west coast of England was different from his homeland, Tomori, with a look that implied this was a question that shouldn't have been asked, said, "Wind is wind anywhere."

Rocca, who had lost the 1995 Open to John Daly in a four-hole play-off, had a practically unblemished scorecard, two bogeys offset by two birdies.

He made only two bad shots, both on par-3 holes — on the fourth, where he missed the green to the right, and on the 12th, where he pulled a one iron into deep grass on a slope left of the green. Both shots cost him strokes. In one of his better-played holes, Rocca scrambled a par 4 on the sixth, where he played a solid drive and followed with an even better three wood and found himself 20 yards short of the green. A nice pitch and a solid putt saved his 4.

Rocca made up for his mistakes with birdies on the third and 17th, and might have made more. He missed makeable putts from six feet on both the 14th, another par-3, and the 15th.

"If I make another round like this one," Rocca said, "I think I make top 10."

Even though Watts not only had held first place but lengthened his lead to two strokes with his 73, Rose remained the gallery's hero. He earned it. After bogeying the first two holes — three-putting the first and one-putting the second for his 5 — Rose ran off seven consecutive pars and made the turn in 36.

Coming home he dropped three strokes quickly — on the 10th, where he three-putted, on the 13th,

Jim Furyk (212) was known as a good player in the wind.

where he drove into a bunker and had no shot at the green, and on the 14th, where he missed the green with a four-iron second. Playing a superb pitch to three feet, Justin took one stroke back by birdieing the 15th, a long par-5 into the wind, and had a chance to save par at the home hole. But after driving into the rough and taking two more to get on, he missed from 12 feet.

As his final putt dropped, the gallery went wild, raising a thunderous roar as the young man shot 75, a better score than just a handful of the professionals. Only 13 men had shot a better round, and only four had a better 54-hole score than his 213.

Playing like a seasoned professional, he had struck some wonderful shots, especially his irons throughout the stretch of seven straight pars. His driver from the sixth fairway was among the best shots struck there throughout the day. It bore through the fierce headwind and raced to the green, setting up a two-putt par, one of only 21 that day.

With the enthusiasm of his youth, Justin called his day "tremendous."

"Starting out I didn't realise it would be anything like that. On every hole I got an ovation. It was incredible, people shouting my name. It pushed me on."

Asked if he knew he had become a famous name in British sport, Rose said, "No, I don't think so. Well, just walking around there today I could see how many people obviously know my name. I don't know what to make of it I guess. I almost sort of saw myself as Jack Nicklaus, for some silly reason. Every time he walks up the 18th hole he gets an ovation. You know, going through anything like that is just incredible."

Rose actually led the championship after Watts bogeyed both the 11th and 12th. Justin stood one over par for the 57 holes then. His lead lasted only the one hole. Watts birdied the 13th, the longest of the par-4s, through a good break. His six-iron approach hit short but bounced onto the green, curled right, and rolled within two feet of the cup.

Watts made that putt, but he had had trouble holing makeable putts throughout the early holes. He missed from seven feet and bogeyed the first,

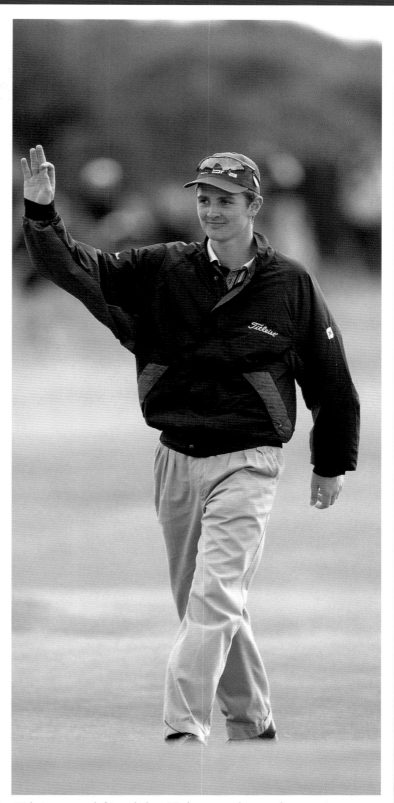

Justin Rose (213) managed only a par 5 on the 17th (sequence left) and shot 75, but came home a hero again.

Thomas Bjorn (215) made 7 on the par-5 15th.

missed another of the same length on the sixth, three-putted the seventh, missing the second from six feet, and missed from five feet on both the 11th and 12th.

He called his birdie on the 13th the turning point of his round. It steadied him enough to par the next three and birdie the 17th, driving with a three wood and playing a six-iron second to 30 feet. There he had a little luck. He caught his six iron a bit thin, but the ball bounced onto the green, and Watts got down in two putts.

Back to level par then, he parred the 18th, shot 73, and finished two strokes clear of the field.

He couldn't relax, though, because he had a number of dangerous men close behind him, and the most serious of those could be Woods and O'Meara — Woods because he could shoot anything at all, and O'Meara because he had already won the Masters. And don't forget that while he had played some shabby stuff in the middle two rounds of the US Open and tied for 32nd, he had closed with 69 over the difficult Olympic Club course.

Those with longer memories recalled that O'Meara finished 68-67-69 at Royal Birkdale in 1991, shot 275, and tied Fred Couples for third place, behind

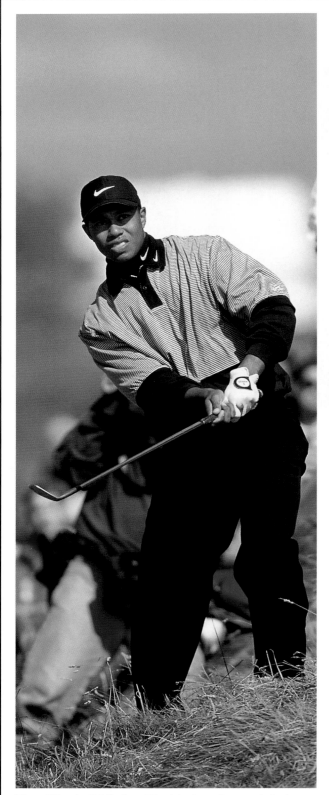

Tiger Woods (215) shot 77 with 6 on the par-4 sixth.

Brad Faxon (215) bogeyed the 16th and 18th holes.

Raymond Russell (216) finished with two 5s.

the Australians Ian Baker-Finch and Mike Harwood. O'Meara had gone into the last round tied with Baker-Finch, but Baker-Finch was unbeatable that week. He closed with 66 against O'Meara's 69 and beat him by three strokes.

O'Meara made the day's most significant move with his 72. At 212, he had climbed within reach of Watts, an untested player at this level of competition. It hadn't been easy, and at two stages O'Meara looked as if he had taken several steps backwards.

Trouble began at the first hole, where he became entangled in the rough twice, couldn't reach the green with his third shot, and made 6. Two strokes were gone, and he now trailed Watts by five strokes, and Brian hadn't played a shot. Another bogey on the fifth, where Mark bunkered his approach, and he still lagged five behind Watts, who had bogeyed the first.

Then O'Meara went on to the sixth, where he became involved in a problem with the Rules of Golf that confused everyone, including the officials, and must have taken 20 minutes to untangle.

At 480 yards, the hole is long enough as it is, but the ground rises as it approaches the green and high

Sandy Lyle (218) had only one birdie.

David Duval (216) started with two bogeys.

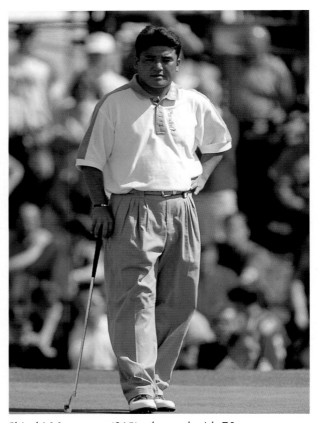

Shigeki Maruyama (218) advanced with 75.

Greg Turner (218) took 6 on the par-4 second.

dunes border both sides. With the wind blustering slightly from the right, O'Meara drove nicely into the fairway, and from roughly 230 yards, realised he would have to play another driver to reach the green. He made solid contact, but he had aimed it slightly right, expecting the wind to bring it back. It didn't. The ball streaked towards the right dune, carried the crest, and disappeared into undergrowth so dense, O'Meara would be lucky to find his ball.

What happened next stemmed from vague wording in the definition of a lost ball. The relevant clause states a ball is lost if "it is not found *or* identified as his by the player within five minutes after the player's side or his or their caddies have begun to search for it."

Most golfers assumed the player himself was compelled to identify his ball within the five minutes, but the word "or" confused the definition. Did it mean that so long as the ball had been found within the allotted time, O'Meara was under no obligation to identify it? This was the crux of a series of debates amongst rules officials.

According to O'Meara's account, this is what happened.

Mark O'Meara (212) hit his second shot on the sixth hole far right, resulting in an extensive search for his golf ball.

By the time he and his caddie reached the dune, spectators had already been looking for it. Pointing to a spot, one of them said, "It hit right here. We saw it hit here and bounce there."

O'Meara said that with 30 or more spectators thrashing through the bushes, he couldn't work his way close enough to look for it himself. "I was looking," he said, "they were looking and tramping and stamping the grass and bushes. I guess maybe three minutes had gone by when I told my caddie, 'Jerry, this isn't looking too good. Give me a ball and I can start walking back.'"

Mark claimed that at this point one official told him his five minutes had lapsed. Even though he believed he still had time left, Mark didn't object, because he assumed that even if he found his ball it was probably unplayable, and two club lengths' relief would do him no good. Most likely he would have to return and play another shot.

He said he had probably walked 30 yards when he heard the gallery shouting, "We've found it," but no one waved for him to come back, so he walked on to where he had played the original shot. (The question now centred on whether the ball had been found

within the five minutes.)

Spectators watching the scene couldn't figure out what spurred the officials' debates. After a short period, O'Meara was waved back to the green. Evidently the R and A next determined the ball was indeed lost, and one of them put O'Meara in a buggy and drove him back out on the fairway. Another huddle and they changed their minds, decided the ball had been found within five minutes and that it wasn't necessary for O'Meara to identify it. He was driven in where the officials huddled once more.

Meantime, O'Meara was saying, "If it's a lost ball, if it's unplayable, or if you want me to play from here or there, I'll play from wherever you want. Just make the call. Whatever way it goes, I hit the shot. I'll live with it."

After yet another conference, the officials agreed O'Meara's ball had been found within the allotted five minutes and that he should play from the undergrowth, lying two.

Now there was a further complication. When one man saw O'Meara walk back out the fairway the first time, he assumed O'Meara had abandoned his ball, and he picked it up. Fortunately, the man didn't

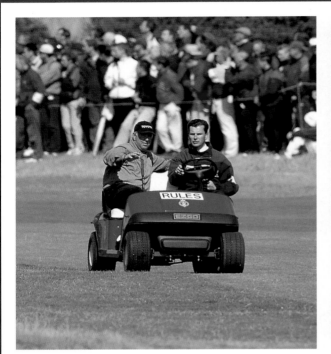

O'Meara's golf ball was found and after several rules discussions, he returned to play his third shot.

He saved par here at the 10th, in the midst of six consecutive pars before his birdie at the 13th.

O'Meara blasted from the back bunker on the 17th to within six feet, and made birdie 4.

move, and when the matter had been settled, he could point to the spot where the ball had lain.

The undergrowth had been above everyone's knees when the search began, but now O'Meara dropped his ball in grass that had been trampled flat. After two drops rolled more than two club lengths, Mark placed his ball, played a nice pitch, and made 5. Had he been forced to play another shot from 230 yards out (it would have been his fourth), he might have made anything.

Discussing the bizarre situation later, O'Meara admitted the spectator did him a favour by picking up the ball. "No question it was a tremendous break," he added. "I was able to get a sand wedge on it, put it on the green, and escape with a 5."

From then on O'Meara made no mistakes. With birdies on the 13th, where he holed from 20 feet, and the 17th, where he recovered from a bunker to six feet, he played the last 12 holes in two under par and salvaged what had begun as a grim day.

Now, as he had been seven years earlier, O'Meara would go into the last round of an Open at Royal Birkdale in position to win.

As for the definition of a lost ball, the ambiguous wording had been spotted by a rules specialist over a year earlier, and it had been under discussion between the R and A and the United States Golf Association ever since. It should be resolved before the Open Championship in 1999.

He shot 72 with 34 on the second nine.

THIRD ROUND RESULTS

HOLE	1	2	3	4	5	6	7	8	9	10	11	12	13	14	15	16	17	18	
PAR	4	4	4	3	4	4	3	4	4	4	4	3	4	3	5	4	5	4	TOTAL
Brian Watts	5	4	4	3	4	5	4	4	4	4	5	4	3	3	5	4	4	4	73-210
Jesper Parnevik	4	4	4	2	4	5	4	4	4	4	4	3	4	3	5	5	4	5	72-212
Jim Furyk	4	5	3	3	5	6	3	4	4	4	4	3	4	3	5	4	4	4	72-212
Mark O'Meara	6	4	4	3	5	5	3	4	4	4	4	3	3	3	5	4	4	4	72-212
*Justin Rose	5	5	4	3	4	4	3	4	4	5	4	3	5	4	4	4	5	5	75-213
John Huston	4	4	4	3	5	4	3	4	4	4	5	3	5	3	5	5	4	4	73-215
Brad Faxon	5	4	4	4	3	5	3	4	4	4	5	3	4	3	5	5	4	5	74-215
Thomas Bjorn	4	4	4	3	3	5	3	4	5	5	4	3	5	3	7	4	5	5	76-215
Tiger Woods	4	4	4	4	5	6	3	4	4	4	4	4	4	4	4	5	4	4	77-215
Katsuyoshi Tomori	4	4	4	3	4	4	3	3	4	4	5	2	4	3	6	5	4	4	70-216
Costantino Rocca	4	4	3	4	4	4	3	4	4	4	4	4	4	3	5	4	5	4	70-216
Raymond Russell	4	5	4	3	4	4	3	4	5	5	4	3	4	3	6	4	5	5	75-216
David Duval	5	5	3	2	5	5	4	4	5	5	4	3	4	3	6	4	4	4	75-216
Gordon Brand Jnr	5	5	5	3	4	5	3	4	4	5	4	3	5	3	5	5	4	4	76-217
Davis Love III	5	5	4	3	4	6	4	4	4	4	5	3	5	4	5	4	4	4	77-217

* Denotes amateur

HOLE SUMMARY

HOLE	PAR	EAGLES	BIRDIES	PARS	BOGEYS	HIGHER	RANK	AVERAGE
1	4	0	2	33	36	10	3	4.69
2	4	0	1	28	44	8	2	4.75
3	4	0	9	57	14	1	17	4.09
4	3	0	8	49	21	3	15	3.24
5	4	0	5	42	30	4	9	4.43
6	4	0	0	21	50	10	1	4.89
7	3	0	2	41	35	3	8	3.48
8	4	0	2	67	12	0	16	4.12
9	4	0	1	50	27	3	11	4.40
OUT	34	0	30	388	269	42		38.09
10	4	0	7	33	34	7	6	4.54
11	4	0	0	38	34	9	5	4.64
12	3	0	4	53	20	4	14	3.30
13	4	0	3	46	27	5	10	4.42
14	3	0	8	41	27	5	12	3.36
15	5	0	3	53	20	5	13	5.33
16	4	0	1	35	35	10	4	4.68
17	5	2	39	29	10	1	18	4.64
18	4	0	2	44	29	6	7	4.49
IN	36	2	67	372	236	52		39.41
TOTAL	70	2	97	760	505	94		77.49

Players Below Par	0
Players At Par	2
Players Above Par	79

LOW SCORES

Low First Nine	Katsuyoshi Tomori	33
Low Second Nine	Mark O'Meara	34
Low Round	Katsuyoshi Tomori	70
	Costantino Rocca	70

WEATHER

Temperature: low 14°C, high 21°C.
Strong, gusty southwest winds.

Playing here into the 18th green, Brian Watts carried a two-stroke lead into the final round.

A LONG JOURNEY TO STARDOM

BY ALISTER NICOL

The Open Championship is rightly regarded as the most cosmopolitan of all golf events. In terms of nationalities represented it far outstrips the other three majors, Masters, US Open and USPGA Championship. Indeed, golfers from no fewer than 20 countries played their way into what eventual winner Mark O'Meara would describe as "the most special championship there is." Whether a certain Korean gentleman would agree is moot. He suffered the indignity of running out of golf balls attempting to survive Final Qualifying and was forced to withdraw. His long journey had been in vain.

Not so for another long-distance traveller. Brian Watts is well-accustomed to the peripatetic life and in a way mirrors the international flavour of golf's oldest championship. Son of an English father and a German mother, he was born in Montreal, raised in Dallas, educated at Oklahoma State University, where he won an NCAA Championship in 1987, and now plays the majority of his golf in Japan. He does very well, too, in a country to which he commutes several times a year from the family home in Edmond, Oklahoma, which he shares with his wife Debbye and year-old son Jason. His was not a household name even there before the Open. The man frequently greeted by strangers on the streets of Tokyo and Yokohama as "Watts-san" is assured of much more recognition now, however, following his Royal Birkdale exploits.

He does not willingly rack up all those air miles. He does it through necessity. The Japanese Tour, for so long a closed shop to all but a fortunate few non-Japanese, is the only one in the world where Watts enjoys full playing privileges.

He entered the USPGA Tour qualifying tournament on five occasions after turning professional in 1988, succeeding in gaining a card only once. He was unable to retain it and headed across the Pacific

to Japan in 1993. Since then, his effortless-looking swing, founded on superb timing and rhythm, has seen him win 11 tournaments and amass what seem truly staggering millions of yen. Converted to dollars they still add up to a lot. He estimates his five victories of 1994 earned him around US$1.4 million, but even that was not enough to buy him a house in Japan.

While he arrived at Royal Birkdale as a relative unknown, he brought with him a fair amount of Open Championship experience, albeit none of a startling nature. This was his sixth successive Open, having made his debut at Royal St George's in 1993. He missed the cut that year, was 55th at Turnberry in 1994, improved to 40th at St Andrews in 1995, but missed the cut in the two subsequent years. All the time he was gaining valuable links experience. It was that experience, allied to a technically sound game and that wonderfully easy swing, which enabled him to shoot 68 and 69 and to go out in the third day's final pairing with new British teenage sensation Justin Rose.

By the time Watts and the 17-year-old amateur boarded the first tee for another day of jousting with the buffeting wind, people were no longer asking "Brian who?" although the previous night his wife, his caddie and his caddie's girlfriend had dined unnoticed in a Southport restaurant. But he had proved to golf's cognoscenti that not only could he play, he could also handle the elements with as much equanimity and skill as anyone in the field.

He seemed in total control, though he had admitted earlier that while mentally he kept insisting to himself that he should be enjoying his tussle with the elements, he simply did not like playing in wind and rain.

His demeanour never once betrayed any indication of inner turmoil. He looked cool, calm and collected

Watts nearly holed this putt for birdie, but settled for 73 in the third round.

every step of the way. It was not always thus, however. Earlier in 1998 he had blown a fuse. Not just once, but twice, in the same day. He had, apparently, been cruising along nicely in the second round of the Fuji Sankei Classic, which he had won in 1996. He seemed assured of making the cut. Yet for reasons not fully established, he deliberately hit a ball into the ocean on the 13th hole thereby incurring penalty shots. Two holes later, according to Japanese golf writers, Brian faced a shot which should have required no more than a wedge to reach the putting surface on the 15th. He elected to hit a three wood. The ball soared high and clear over the green and into the water. More penalty strokes were to be added. The cut comfortably missed, the American then had to face the ire of Japanese officialdom. The PGA fined him £1,000 and the Japanese Golf Association banned him from the 1998 Japan Open.

At Royal Birkdale, Watts declined to discuss the matter. He confined himself to saying, "That all happened two and a half months ago. I made a mistake and I'm sorry. It's now history." When he and Rose embarked on their third round, Watts was fully aware that he could be making more history.

No player from the Japanese Tour had ever won an Open and no one had a better chance than himself.

Watts' playing partner, Rose, had an army of fans ready to swarm over Royal Birkdale's dunes and give their new hero ear-splitting support. Such partisanship did not upset the quiet American in the slightest. Quite the opposite. "To be honest I wish I was him," Watts said after shooting 73 to the youngster's 75. "It was a lot of fun to watch and listen to the reaction from the gallery to Justin's play. Every time he came to the tee box, or walked down the fairway, or came to the green, or holed a putt, the crowd was ecstatic. It was a pleasure to watch it. He's what, 17 or 18? He's a marvellous player, fabulous. He'll be holding the claret jug some day, I'm sure. He's an outstanding player. We had a really good time out there today. A little chit-chat here and there and complimenting each other. We had a lot of fun."

It was not all fun, however. The elements saw to that. And Watt's professionalism shone through on a day when the hopes of many more celebrated golfers were literally blown away. In the main he refused to raise his eyes towards the giant leaderboards scattered across Royal Birkdale's links. He commented afterwards, "I didn't see a leaderboard too many times. I was too busy trying to figure out if I could hit a green, how much wind to play, trying to stay steady on my putts. There was a lot going through my mind without looking at leaderboards."

At the end of yet another gruelling day, however, his name was right up there at the very top. At level par for three rounds he was in the exalted, and totally unaccustomed, position of leading the Open.

The carnage inflicted upon many in the third round is fully documented elsewhere. Suffice to say scores in the 80s were commonplace and only two players, Katsuyoshi Tomori from Japan and Costantino Rocca, managed to match the par of 70. Interestingly, Tomori has almost done a Watts in reverse, career-wise. He has left his native tour to become the first Japanese to join the PGA European Tour. He also seems to share the American's ability to stoically accept whatever weather conditions the golfing gods elect to hurl at players. When asked if the wind howling in across the Lancashire coast from off the Irish Sea was worse than any he had encountered in, say, Okinawa, he smiled politely and replied, "Wind is wind … anywhere. It still blows."

For three long, tough days Watts proved to the world and, perhaps more significantly, to his fellow competitors that he was as good a wind player as there is. Some much more experienced players grumbled and groaned that in the conditions the course was too severe, that some tees might have been forward, that it bordered on the unfair, was "almost unplayable." Watts disagreed. Asked if that was how he saw the conditions from his lofty perch, he replied with a curt, "Absolutely not. I believe when the conditions are as tough as this what will happen tomorrow, in the final round, is that the strongest person mentally is going to win. I've never led a major with a round to go, so I don't know how I'll feel. But I know this much. There is not one let-up hole on this course in conditions as tough as this. You don't have time to kind of take a break and just enjoy. You don't have one shot out there that's easy."

For 54 holes Brian Watts found it easier than the remainder of the field.

What he will find less easy is deciding where his

Watts earned a place on the USPGA Tour.

future lies after a week when people stopped asking "Brian who?" His gallant defeat in the four-hole play-off by Mark O'Meara earned him a host of new admirers and a cheque for £188,000. That's sure to be more than enough to guarantee playing privileges on the USPGA Tour, which he admits is his dream. But, being an honourable man, he is grateful for the opportunities afforded him by the Japanese Tour and the contracts he has over there. He makes a tidy living but he does miss his wife and son. Wherever he decides his future lies, one thing is certain: Golf's ultimate travellin' man will not be able to eat incognito at Carnoustie when he comes to the 128th Open.

Mark O'Meara (280) holed a 16-foot birdie putt here at the eighth, and said later, "That was huge."

O'MEARA ENDURES IN PLAY-OFF

BY ROBERT SOMMERS

In the last rounds of the Masters, the US Open and the Open, Mark O'Meara's game changed. While in the past he had built a resume of indifferent closing rounds, all at once he converted himself into a strong finisher by closing all three championships with rounds in the 60s. Chronologically, he shot 67 and won the Masters, shot 69 but tied for 32nd in the US Open, and shot 68, which won the Open on a stirring final that thrilled the galleries at Royal Birkdale and tested both the shotmaking and the resolve of those lurking close to the top when the day began. Until 1998, he had finished with a round in the 60s in only three of 13 Opens, one of 16 US Opens, two of 15 USPGA Championships, and he had never finished with a sub-70 score in 13 Masters.

Suddenly O'Meara had reversed his pattern. Where he had played dull golf in the past, now he made birdies when they mattered. In those three final rounds he birdied 17 holes, a fraction less than six in each, and in all 12 rounds he shot five scores in the 60s.

He had won at Augusta by birdieing the last three holes, and he had claimed the 127th Open Championship with one birdie on the 17th and another on the first of the four play-off holes, after he finished with 68 for a level-par 280 total.

Brian Watts, the surprising third-round leader, held on through the regulation 72 holes, finishing with 70, but he missed two makeable putts on the first play-off holes and couldn't recover, losing with 19 strokes to O'Meara's 17 over the four holes.

By winning the Open, O'Meara had blossomed into one of the game's most dangerous players. At the age of 41, it had taken him a long time.

O'Meara first surfaced in 1979, when he beat John Cook, the defender, in the US Amateur at Canterbury Golf Club, in Cleveland, then joined the USPGA Tour in 1981, the year he played in his first Open.

Since 1980, while he was still an amateur, he had played in 57 of the game's most important four championships and hadn't won one of them. He had not challenged the leaders more than six or seven times, although notably in the 1991 Open, again at Royal Birkdale. O'Meara tied for third, three strokes behind Ian Baker-Finch, who, incidentally, beat him by three strokes in the last round. He had also tied for third in his second Open, at Sandwich, in 1985. Had he shot 69 at Sandwich, he would have won, but with 72 he finished two strokes behind Sandy Lyle, who, again, beat him by two strokes in the closing round.

Obviously he liked Royal Birkdale. In two Opens, he had shot five rounds in the 60s and had never slipped above 72. He shot 71-68-67-69–275 in 1991, and 72-68-72-68–280 under considerably worse weather in 1998.

His was a landmark victory. A man who had been a consistent winner through 17 years of professional golf but who seemed to lack whatever it took on the big occasions, O'Meara abruptly established himself as a winner of championships.

Looking at his record, no one could be sure if his winning the Masters had been a fluke. The last round at Royal Birkdale would test him because, as it had been at Augusta, once again he would have to make up ground. He came into the climactic round two strokes behind Watts, who was playing as if leading the Open was something he did every day. He showed no signs of nervousness, even though he was being chased by some of the game's most dangerous men.

Rather than O'Meara, some believed Tiger Woods was the most dangerous of all. Reeling from his third-round 77, Woods had looked everyone in the eye and said, "I'm in pretty good shape. Right now I'm only five back. I have to go out tomorrow, post a good round, and see what happens."

Jim Furyk (282) was let down by his putting.

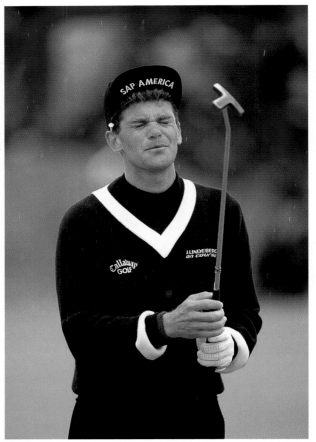

Jesper Parnevik (282) couldn't overcome three poor drives.

Reflecting on the weather, Woods added, "If the conditions tomorrow are like this, or more difficult, it would be best for the guys who are behind, because you know if you can shoot even par, or one or two under if you're really playing well, you have a great chance of winning. If it's calm, you would have to shoot 63 or 64."

Bravado perhaps, but Tiger had it just about right.

While the wind slackened off and blew in from a different direction the next day, a dull, gray overcast hid the sky, periodic rains fell, and the 37,000 spectators caught no more than an occasional glimpse of sunlight.

In the more forgiving atmosphere, Woods went round Royal Birkdale in 66 and posted a score of 281, one over par, while O'Meara and Watts still had holes to play. It was a marvellous round, but Woods had calculated correctly. He needed that 64. One stroke behind, Woods took third place.

Even in milder weather, Royal Birkdale gave no ground. Only nine men shot in the 60s, and just seven others shot level-par 70. Along with Woods,

Raymond Russell (282) charged to a fourth-place tie with 66, having four birdies and no bogeys.

Raymond Russell, a 25-year-old Scot, with his own 66, shared the low round of the day.

Some others improved on ruinous rounds the previous day. Davis Love III shot 68 and climbed to eighth place after his 77 of Saturday, and Justin Leonard closed out a disappointing defence of his championship by shooting 69, bouncing back from a horrid 82 in the third round. US Open champion Lee Janzen recovered from 80 with a closing 70, Sven Struver went from 80 to 68, and Nick Price rebounded from his lethal 82 with 72.

Perhaps disheartened after their battering in Saturday's gale, some others might have unconsciously let down. Dudley Hart played the last two rounds in 85-80 and finished last, Mark Brooks closed 75-80, Andrew Oldcorn 84-79, Phil Mickelson 85-78, and reliable Fred Couples stumbled through the last two rounds in 78-81.

Meantime, the last round opened with serious questions about O'Meara, Watts, Woods and Justin Rose.

The darling of the galleries, Rose stood on ground very few others had walked. Not since Young Tom

Davis Love III (285) was in eighth place alone.

Brian Watts (280) played level par through 11.

Morris won the Open 130 years ago had a 17-year-old come to the last round of the Open with the championship within reach. Could he hold up to the physical and mental rigours of golf at this level?

Watts, who lost his eligibility to play the USPGA Tour, had led the previous two rounds and faced the same demons. Would he hold up under the pressure without fraying his nerve ends?

Then there was Woods. Only 22 years of age, Tiger had shown he could shoot any score at all, but since he won the 1997 Masters, in the major championships he had shot those scores either too early or too late. Could he make up the five strokes he needed, as Leonard had done a year earlier?

O'Meara had already proved himself by his stunning finish at Augusta, birdieing the last three holes to snatch the Masters from Couples and David Duval. Besides, he had that liking for Royal Birkdale. In his first tournament there, he won the 1987 Lawrence Batley International, a PGA European Tour event.

Every one of the four played a role in the final round on a day when eight men could have won — Watts, O'Meara, Woods, Rose, Russell, Jesper Parnevik, Jim Furyk and Brad Faxon. All had to make something happen, but only O'Meara did enough. Like Woods, beginning five strokes behind Watts, Faxon lost three further strokes through the eighth and dropped back; Parnevik and Furyk played steady par golf but needed more, and the irrepressible Rose smiled his way to 69 and 282, tied for fourth place with Parnevik, Furyk and Russell. It was the best finish by an amateur in the Open since 1953, when America Frank Stranahan tied for second behind Ben Hogan.

After 16 holes, Russell was still in the hunt, but he needed two birdies for 281, or an eagle and a birdie for 280. Reaching the 17th green with his second, he had a chance for the eagle but birdied instead, then parred the 18th.

Still, he was the surprise of the day, even more so than young Rose. A 25-year-old Scot, Russell matched Woods' 66, the best rounds of the day, and was beaten by only three men in a year when, stricken with hepatitis, he had missed 12 cuts in 14 tournaments. He had finished over par in 13 of those, and broke par by four strokes only in the Deutsch Bank SAP Open, in Hamburg. Even so, he finished tied for 67th.

It is interesting to speculate how the championship might have developed had Woods birdied three of the first four holes instead of three of the last four. Had Tiger begun with a rush, he might have sent ripples through the rest of the field and perhaps upset their tempos. Instead, by the time he made his move, Parnevik and Furyk had lost their chances, and Watts and O'Meara were fighting it out between them. Woods could only hope both stumbled at the end. As for his effect on Rose, it seems entirely unlikely anyone would have unnerved that precocious young man.

Playing in the third from last group, Rose stepped onto the first tee to thundering applause from the gallery, and promptly pulled his tee shot into the left rough, played short of the green with his second, and bogeyed. As his putt glided past the hole, he shrugged his shoulders and grinned.

Nothing upset his composure. Whenever the gallery cheered him, he waved. He shook every hand he could reach, and occasionally signed autographs. As he strode along, an aeroplane droned overhead towing the message, "Go, Justin." Teen-aged girls and boys waved bed sheets flaunting his name.

With all the distractions, Rose nevertheless kept his mind on his game. He birdied the short fourth with a glorious shot to 10 feet, but then lost strokes by bunkering his tee shot on the seventh and going from one rough to the other on the eighth. He finished the first nine in 36, two over par.

Justin played much steadier golf coming back, pulling himself back to level par for the round by holing from 12 feet on the 12th, then reaching the 15th green with a drive and three wood and getting down in two from 35 feet.

Rose had fought back to three over par for the championship then, and he could catch Woods, who had finished, by birdieing both the 17th and 18th. All hope collapsed when he could do no more than par the 17th, but he finished with a flourish. His five iron from the rough at the last pulled up short and in more heavy grass, but his pitch cleared a bunker,

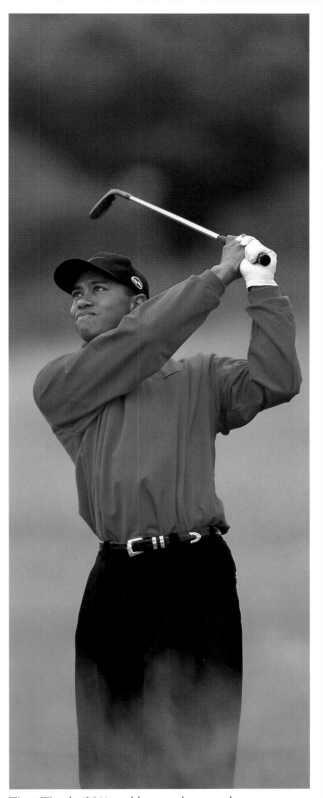

Tiger Woods (281) could not make an early move.

Woods birdied three of the final four, including this dramatic pitch-in from 30 feet on the 17th hole.

then ran into the hole for a birdie 3.

The roar echoed throughout the golf course and possibly into Southport, off to the north. Rose had come back in 33, three under par, shot 69 and 282, and finished better than any British amateur since Roger Wethered tied Jock Hutchison for first place in 1921. Hutchison won the play-off.

Rose had played golf beyond his age. Over the four days he had shot two rounds in the 60s, eagled the 17th during his second-round 66, birdied 12 holes, parred 43, and bogeyed 16. Never once did he lose more than one stroke on any hole, astonishing for one so young.

Meantime, as the gallery gloried in their new hero, others decided the championship.

Woods had already thrilled the gallery with his powerful finish. He had staggered through the first hole, rolling his first bold putt eight feet past, missing the second, and then tapping in his third with a stroke that caused the R and A to look at the video tape. Some suggested Woods scraped the ball into the cup rather than "fairly striking" the ball, as the rules demand. The R and A said Tiger had violated no rule.

Quickly, he pitched to 15 feet and birdied the second, played a glorious 200-yard downwind eight iron to six feet and birdied the fourth, overshot the sixth with a three-iron second and bogeyed, then rifled a six iron to one foot and birdied the eighth.

With two bogeys he had gone out in 33, one under par.

He made no more bogeys on the second nine, but he stood four over par after the 14th, behind not only Watts and O'Meara, but Parnevik, Furyk and Russell as well. He needed birdies.

He began making them on the 15th, where he played a tremendous 270-yard three wood from gnarly rough to the edge of the green. He got down in two. Three under par now, Woods went on to the 17th, where he holed a 30-foot chip from over the green. He was two over. Now came the 18th, where he holed another 30-footer. He had come back in 33. With 281, one over par, he could only wait to see if his finish had any effect.

Watts, meantime, had played as steadily as ever. After running off three pars, he three-putted the fourth from 30 feet but birdied the fifth from 35 feet. When four more pars took him to the ninth in 34, level par, he still led O'Meara by two strokes.

Playing a hole ahead of Watts, O'Meara, meantime, had found trouble on the sixth once again. His approach hit a slope at the edge of the green and caromed sharply into the same kind of knee-high grass as his second shot the previous day, except this grass hadn't been tramped down. A good chip saved a bogey.

Level par for the day, O'Meara slipped to one over by overshooting the seventh, but then had a lucky

Justin Rose (282) concluded his almost magical performance by holing out at the 18th for birdie 3.

Watts had his right foot out of the bunker at the 18th.

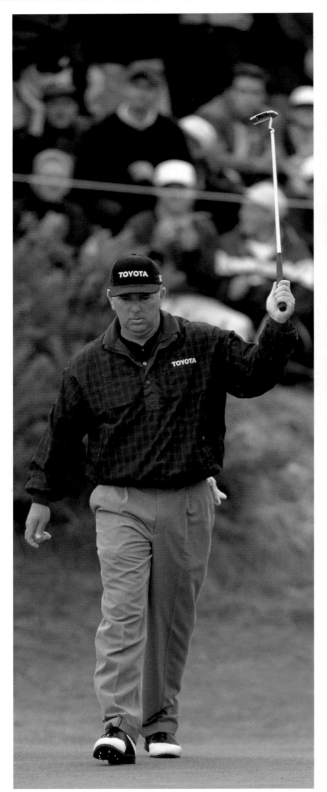

O'Meara birdied the 17th from 15 feet after a poor drive.

break on the eighth. From an awkward lie in the left rough, with the ball well below his feet, O'Meara's pitch missed the green to the right, scooted up a mound, ran through some heavy stuff at the top, curled left, caught a closely cropped downslope, and trickled down to the green, hole high. He holed the putt for an unexpected birdie.

O'Meara passed Watts by birdieing both the 11th and 12th, holing solid putts from 15 and 22 feet, while Watts missed the 12th green badly, pushing his tee shot into tall grass behind a mound. He was lucky to bogey. Now O'Meara stood at level par and Watts, one over.

At about the same time Watts was bogeying 12, O'Meara pulled his approach to the 13th into a greenside bunker and bogeyed as well. They were tied at one over par.

O'Meara jumped ahead once more by ripping a three iron hole high about four feet right of the 14th and birdieing again. While Watts kept grinding out pars, O'Meara dropped another stroke on the 16th, pulling his approach shot and misreading his putt. They were tied again, but once more O'Meara

From that awkward stance, Watts executed an almost perfect bunker shot that stopped a foot or so from the hole.

birdied. A drive drifted into the rough on the 17th, but he hacked it out with one nine iron, followed by another nine iron to about 15 feet, and holed the putt. He was level par. Minutes later, Watts birdied the 17th as well, and then played a remarkable bunker shot to save himself on the 18th. His second shot, played from the left rough, landed quite a bit short of the green, but it had come out of the grass with a lot of run and rolled into an awkward position in the left greenside bunker.

From a downslope, with his right foot out of the bunker, Watts would have to carry over the bunker's arching front face and let it run to the hole. It was as difficult a shot as anyone could imagine, especially for a man who had never played under such tension.

Watts played it perfectly. He chopped down, the ball shot up, cleared the bunker face, hit the green running, and died little more than one foot from the cup, for a heart-stopping moment looking as if it might fall.

It was one of the finest bunker shots ever at a critical moment of a major championship. It rivalled Bobby Jones' pitch from a bunker on the 17th at

Hoylake in the 1930 Open, Bob Tway's pitch into the 18th hole at Inverness when he snatched the 1986 USPGA Championship from Greg Norman, and Sandy Lyle's shot onto Augusta's 18th that set up a birdie to win the 1988 Masters. Watching with the gallery, O'Meara applauded.

Now the two men were tied at 280. Woods had been eliminated and they would decide the championship between them in a four-hole play-off beginning at Birkdale's 15th hole, the par-5.

Watts played the better shots into the first two greens, but twice he missed the putts. O'Meara birdied the 15th, and with three more pars won the play-off.

Watts had played wonderfully, never losing control of his game until a few loose drives on the play-off holes, but he had been up against one of the game's best ball-strikers, a man who had suddenly learned to win on the big occasions.

By winning, O'Meara emerged as a formidable golfer at an age when most others wilt away. This was his second major championship of the year, linking him with six others who had won both the

O'Meara (left) hit his third shot close for birdie at the 15th, the first play-off hole, then Watts missed his birdie try.

Watts saved par at the 17th after driving in the rough.

Masters and the Open in the same year. At age 41, he was not only the oldest of those seven, but the oldest to have won two or more of the Open, the US Open, the Masters and the USPGA in a single year. Hogan, in 1953, and Jack Nicklaus, in 1980, were 40 years of age. Nicklaus won the US Open and USPGA, and Hogan won the Masters, US Open and the Open.

O'Meara won by playing his best golf when it counted most. He played the last 11 holes in three under par, and holed a critical putt on the 17th after nearly giving the championship away. He had persisted through one of the Open's more gripping finishes, ending as the galleries cheered themselves hoarse watching a series of dramatic finishes, first Woods' inspired 66 that thrust him into a contending position, then Rose's unlikely pitch into the 18th hole that brought him within a stroke of Woods, then Watts' unreal bunker shot on the 18th.

The victory was especially fulfilling for O'Meara, who had laboured on the USPGA Tour for 17 years before winning any of the four major titles. He had been close at times, but he had never seemed to have a game big enough to win. Now, though, with two victories in the same year, O'Meara stood at the top of the game.

Watts came to the 18th in the play-off, knowing he must hole this bunker shot for birdie 3. He made a bogey instead.

Then O'Meara had two putts for his par to win the Open Championship by two strokes.

After hitting his drive on the 18th in the play-off, O'Meara told his caddie, Jerry Higgenbotham, that he had never felt so calm.

"To be honest, I cannot explain it," O'Meara said. "I gave it a good try ... and I did not want to be disappointed today."

FOURTH ROUND RESULTS

HOLE	1	2	3	4	5	6	7	8	9	10	11	12	13	14	15	16	17	18	TOTAL
PAR	4	4	4	3	4	4	3	4	4	4	4	3	4	3	5	4	5	4	TOTAL
Mark O'Meara	4	4	4	2	4	5	4	3	4	4	3	2	5	2	5	5	4	4	68-280
															4	4	5	4	17
Brian Watts	4	4	4	4	3	4	3	4	4	4	4	4	4	3	5	4	4	4	70-280
															5	4	5	5	19
Tiger Woods	5	3	4	2	4	5	3	3	4	4	4	3	4	3	4	4	4	3	66-281
Raymond Russell	4	4	3	3	4	4	4	4	4	4	4	3	4	2	4	4	4	4	66-282
*Justin Rose	5	4	4	2	4	4	4	5	4	4	4	2	4	3	4	4	5	3	69-282
Jim Furyk	4	4	4	4	3	4	3	4	4	4	4	2	4	3	6	4	5	4	70-282
Jesper Parnevik	4	4	4	3	4	5	2	5	3	4	4	3	5	3	5	4	4	4	70-282
Davis Love III	3	3	4	3	5	4	4	4	4	3	4	4	3	3	4	4	5	4	68-285
Costantino Rocca	5	4	3	3	5	4	3	4	4	4	4	3	4	3	4	3	6	4	70-286
Thomas Bjorn	4	4	5	4	4	4	3	4	4	3	4	3	4	3	5	4	5	4	71-286
David Duval	4	4	4	3	4	5	3	4	4	5	3	3	4	4	5	4	4	4	71-287
Brad Faxon	4	4	4	3	4	5	4	5	4	3	5	3	4	3	5	3	5	4	72-287
John Huston	5	4	4	3	3	4	5	3	4	4	3	3	5	3	7	3	5	4	72-287
Gordon Brand Jnr	4	4	3	3	4	4	3	5	3	3	4	3	5	4	7	4	4	4	71-288

* Denotes amateur

HOLE SUMMARY

HOLE	PAR	EAGLES	BIRDIES	PARS	BOGEYS	HIGHER	RANK	AVERAGE
1	4	0	10	40	30	1	5	4.27
2	4	0	8	61	11	1	13	4.06
3	4	0	7	58	14	2	8	4.15
4	3	0	12	54	13	2	13	3.06
5	4	0	10	61	8	2	15	4.03
6	4	0	4	43	31	3	2	4.44
7	3	0	7	55	18	1	7	3.16
8	4	0	4	41	33	3	3	4.43
9	4	0	11	53	17	0	12	4.07
OUT	34	0	73	466	175	15		35.68
10	4	0	16	57	7	1	17	3.91
11	4	0	11	52	16	2	10	4.11
12	3	0	8	42	22	9	4	3.40
13	4	0	4	36	33	8	1	4.56
14	3	0	8	56	14	3	8	3.15
15	5	0	21	47	9	4	16	4.95
16	4	0	10	54	15	2	10	4.11
17	5	0	22	52	4	3	18	4.86
18	4	0	7	54	16	4	6	4.21
IN	36	0	107	450	136	36		37.26
TOTAL	70	0	180	916	311	51		72.94

Players Below Par	9		
Players At Par	7		
Players Above Par	65		

LOW SCORES

Low First Nine	Curtis Strange	31
Low Second Nine	Tiger Woods	33
	Raymond Russell	33
	*Justin Rose	33
Low Round	Tiger Woods	66
	Raymond Russell	66

WEATHER

Temperature: low 14°C, high 23°C.
3.6mm rain, moderate southeast winds.

CHAMPIONSHIP HOLE SUMMARY

HOLE	PAR	YARDS	EAGLES	BIRDIES	PARS	BOGEYS	HIGHER	RANK	AVERAGE
1	4	449	0	29	219	196	28	2	4.49
2	4	421	0	40	282	133	17	7	4.28
3	4	407	0	58	337	74	3	17	4.05
4	3	203	0	53	312	97	10	15	3.14
5	4	344	1	49	310	99	13	14	4.16
6	4	480	0	16	196	219	41	1	4.62
7	3	177	0	35	306	124	7	9	3.22
8	4	457	0	33	331	97	11	13	4.18
9	4	411	0	45	289	131	7	10	4.21
OUT	34	3349	1	358	2582	1170	137		36.35
10	4	403	0	45	295	113	19	8	4.24
11	4	408	0	37	268	137	30	4	4.35
12	3	183	0	39	318	99	16	11	3.20
13	4	498	0	36	266	144	26	6	4.34
14	3	198	0	41	313	107	11	12	3.19
15	5	544	5	82	286	79	20	16	5.06
16	4	416	0	34	268	142	28	4	4.35
17	5	547	27	196	206	35	8	18	4.59
18	4	472	0	31	272	142	27	3	4.37
IN	36	3669	32	541	2492	998	185		37.68
TOTAL 70		7018	33	899	5074	2168	322		74.03

	FIRST ROUND	SECOND ROUND	THIRD ROUND	FOURTH ROUND	TOTAL
Players Below Par	27	7	0	9	43
Players At Par	14	7	2	7	30
Players Above Par	115	140	79	65	399

RELATIVE DIFFICULTY OF HOLES

HOLE	PAR	YARDS	FIRST ROUND	SECOND ROUND	THIRD ROUND	FOURTH ROUND	OVERALL RANK
1	4	449	1	3	3	5	2
2	4	421	8	6	2	13	7
3	4	407	10	17	17	8	17
4	3	203	15	11	15	13	15
5	4	344	12	15	9	15	14
6	4	480	3	1	1	2	1
7	3	177	10	9	8	7	9
8	4	457	14	11	16	3	13
9	4	411	13	5	11	12	10
10	4	403	6	6	6	17	8
11	4	408	5	4	5	10	4
12	3	183	16	13	14	4	11
13	4	498	4	16	10	1	6
14	3	198	9	14	12	8	12
15	5	544	17	10	13	16	16
16	4	416	7	2	4	10	4
17	5	547	18	18	18	18	18
18	4	472	2	8	7	6	3

"I used to wonder what elements were missing," O'Meara said. "Could I not deal with the pressure?"

COMMENTARY

A NEW LEVEL OF SUCCESS

BY JOHN HOPKINS

Are champions born or made? This is one of those questions that have exercised people for years and will continue to do so while competitiveness is a part of our lives. The answer is that some are born and some are made.

For example, Jack Nicklaus and Severiano Ballesteros were born for greatness. One was given an enduring talent that has been unprecedented in golf; the other has been in receipt of a natural genius that flowered young and bloomed spectacularly before withering.

Tiger Woods, on the other hand, may be said to have been made, a prodigy whose almost every move was predetermined by his father from the moment he returned home from the hospital where he was born to be welcomed by the sounds of jazz. Earl Woods did everything he could to produce a champion, and so did Kutilda, his wife.

Likewise Se Ri Pak, the Korean star who has burst upon women's professional golf with the force of a brick hurled through a window, is another who owes a huge amount of her precocity to her parents. She, too, has been made in her father's mould.

Yet there is another category, one for those who are neither born, like Nicklaus, nor made, like Woods. In this category are those like Mark O'Meara, who move along in the foothills of the game until chance elevates them to a level they never expected to reach. Men such as O'Meara do not seek greatness but have it "thrust upon them." Not once but twice within the space of three months, as it happens. All this at age 41. Don't talk to him about a mid-life crisis.

O'Meara has a very precise view of his own position in golf's pantheon. "I think I am a very nice player, a good player. I do not classify myself as a great player. Great players are players like Jack Nicklaus, Byron Nelson and Ben Hogan. I mean players who have won a lot of major championships, have been incredible ambassadors for the game."

Nicklaus and Woods were moulded by the twin influences of prodigious talents that burgeoned so young and determined parents. Ben Hogan was driven to succeed by a desire not to fail, a desire that burned within him so intensely he dared not fail. But O'Meara has found his destiny as a double champion as a result of trying to assist in the development and guidance of another, none other than Woods. It is as if through Woods, he has found his true self.

The making of O'Meara began when O'Meara took on an informal role as adviser and mentor to his young friend. Woods moved to a house in an exclusive gated compound in Orlando, Florida, where O'Meara was already a resident. Baseball star Ken Griffey Jnr lives on the same complex, so does Lee Janzen, the 1998 US Open champion.

How does one describe the relationship between O'Meara, who is almost precisely twice as old as Woods, and his young colleague? Friends? Certainly. Like a father and son? Not at all. Oldest brother with his youngest sibling? Yes. O'Meara helps Woods on the course and from time to time he has helped Woods off it as well. This is what older brothers are supposed to do, isn't it?

Little did O'Meara know as he went through this pastoral work that while Woods was benefiting from his advice, he was benefiting as well. Slowly he was beginning to believe in himself. The ways in which he was helping Woods were causing him to re-examine himself. He had 14 tournament victories and nearly US$9 million in prize money from his 17-year career but, specifically, he wondered why, after 57 professional major championships, he had never won one.

"I used to lie awake at night and wonder what elements were missing," O'Meara said. "Could I not deal with the pressure? Did I lack the stomach to win? Or the heart? I consider myself to be a consistent player who tries to do his best at all times. But then it dawned on me that this was also a valuable talent and all those years of waiting were preparing me for something.

"I don't always hit the ball perfectly, but what I have learned to do is to hang in there when the going gets tough. I may not have the perfect golf swing, but I use past experience to my advantage. When I am near the lead and get nervous, I realise that in the past I had been unable to finish off the deal and get the job done. I had won other tournaments under pressure. I could not figure out why it never happened in the majors."

It took time for O'Meara's self-belief to grow, but the more he played with Woods and the more he helped Woods, the more he was helping himself. It all started to fall into place this year, several years after he had met Woods. The first sign that O'Meara was a man transformed came on a sunny spring evening when he snatched victory in the Masters by one stroke. Then came Royal Birkdale.

O'Meara moved stealthily through the field, starting with a round that was seven strokes worse than Woods and John Huston. A 68 on Friday, while only two under par, was played before the weather was at its worst. It was, in O'Meara's own words, one of the better of the 52 rounds he had played in the Open since he first entered the game's oldest championships at Sandwich in 1981.

This was one day when he demonstrated the maturity and patience necessary to do well in an Open. "The weather can change on a dime," O'Meara said. "To me, that tests the players' ability with their golf swing and to be able to hit different types of strokes. It really tests your composure mentally. To play well round here you have to do a little bit of everything. You're going to miss the greens out there even though the greens are fairly large. You've got to have a good short game. It really makes all the shots in your bag come out and you've got to play them. That is why it is a great championship."

In Saturday's third round O'Meara had the stroke of luck that accompanies champions. On a wild and windy day when Janzen had an 80, Nick Price an 82, Phil Mickelson an 85, O'Meara's 72 took him to two over par, two strokes behind Brian Watts. It might have been worse because O'Meara thought he had lost his ball on the sixth and might have taken a 7. He was walking back to play another when his ball was found and picked up by a spectator.

This was a stroke of luck for O'Meara as officials ruled the spectator was an outside agency and thus O'Meara was given a free drop near where his ball had been found. Two attempts to drop the ball did not work, so O'Meara was able to place it and from there he pitched and two-putted for a 5.

"Do you think Americans still enjoy playing in the Open when the conditions are as bad as they are today?" O'Meara was asked. His response contained precisely the sort of wisdom that Woods had come to appreciate and that has made O'Meara one of the most respected professionals in the US.

"I would hope so," O'Meara replied. "If they don't, I think they will miss the boat. It is one thing to play in benign conditions on an easy golf course. It is another thing to go out and play when the conditions are severe. You know you are not going to get the best breaks all the time. You are going to be unlucky. It tests your patience and you just keep telling yourself, 'Hey, everybody has to deal with this. It is the same course for everybody else.' It is a great championship."

Late in the day of his victory at Royal Birkdale, when it had not really sunk in and the flight aboard Woods' aeroplane back to Orlando the next morning was still 12 hours away, O'Meara admitted how much of his improvement was due to trying to help Tiger.

"Tiger has rejuvenated me," O'Meara said. "Our relationship has been good for both sides. I admire Tiger tremendously. He has been a tremendous asset to the game. Our friendship is a unique one. If I can help teach Tiger, if he can confide in me if he has difficulties or problems with certain areas, I'm more than happy with that.

"He has been a driving force. I just love playing golf with somebody that's a good player. It's like tennis in that you always want to play with someone better. At times I look at Tiger's talent and his tech-

The O'Meara family and the claret jug: Mark and Alicia, son Shuan and daughter Michelle.

nique and his swing and I think he is a better player than I am. That motivated me.

"He has pushed me a little bit. He always keeps saying 'Gosh.' He keeps telling my friends, 'You know Mark can really play and he doesn't get the recognition he deserves.'

"I enjoy playing with Tiger. If he's not the best player in the world he's right there, he and Ernie Els. I think you always enjoy playing with talented people and Tiger is a very talented player and he happens to be a close friend of mine. We play a lot of practice rounds, a lot of golf when we're at home."

O'Meara and Woods often play practice rounds together before major championships. O'Meara, considered by Woods to be one of the best putters in the world, lent Woods his back-up putter and with it, Woods had a 62 at Grand Cypress in Florida just before the Open. It was to help Tiger that he and O'Meara made that pre-Open pilgrimage to some of the great courses in Ireland, to Ballybunion, Waterville and the K Club, and when O'Meara talked about golf in Britain Woods listened. But in doing all this for Woods, O'Meara was doing things that were helping to turn himself into a double champion.

"Coming over here a week early has helped me in the past," Woods admitted during the Open. "When I came over here and played in the Scottish Open as an amateur twice over at Carnoustie, I really enjoyed it because you get acclimatised to this weather. Back in the States it's a little hotter than this right now, especially in Orlando.

"I think it was probably best to come over here. We relaxed. We fished over in Ireland. We played golf. Unfortunately the golf got in the way of the fishing. That was the mind-set we all had last week, just to stay relaxed, prepare, also understand that you don't want to peak last week, you want to peak this week and not stress yourself out."

On the final day Woods and O'Meara demonstrated how much they had both benefited from their friendship with each other. Woods, who had been five strokes behind at the start of the day, produced a stunning finish, birdieing three of his last four holes including a chip-in on the 17th and holing a 30-foot putt across the 18th green for a 66. O'Meara made a 68 look if not easy, then not particularly difficult. Both in that round and in the play-off, his focus never wavered, his swing remained true to the end.

"I have been very fortunate, very blessed to have played this game for a long period," O'Meara said. "I have made a lot of friends, seen a lot of interesting things. Now to take my game to this level at 41 … My family is supportive, I have a supportive wife, Alicia, and two children and that is why I think I play such good golf."

That and acting as a mentor to Tiger Woods.

Justin Leonard (1997)

Nick Faldo (1987, 1990, 1992)

Tom Lehman (1996)

John Daly (1995)

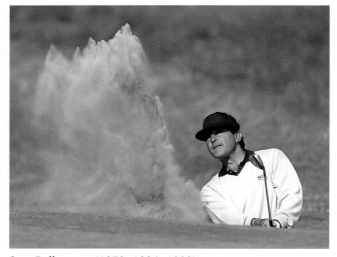

Seve Ballesteros (1979, 1984, 1988)

OPEN CHAMPIONSHIP

YEAR	CHAMPION	SCORE	MARGIN	RUNNERS-UP	VENUE
1860	Willie Park	174	2	Tom Morris Snr	Prestwick
1861	Tom Morris Snr	163	4	Willie Park	Prestwick
1862	Tom Morris Snr	163	13	Willie Park	Prestwick
1863	Willie Park	168	2	Tom Morris Snr	Prestwick
1864	Tom Morris Snr	167	2	Andrew Strath	Prestwick
1865	Andrew Strath	162	2	Willie Park	Prestwick
1866	Willie Park	169	2	David Park	Prestwick
1867	Tom Morris Snr	170	2	Willie Park	Prestwick
1868	Tom Morris Jnr	157	2	Robert Andrew	Prestwick
1869	Tom Morris Jnr	154	3	Tom Morris Snr	Prestwick
1870	Tom Morris Jnr	149	12	Bob Kirk, David Strath	Prestwick
1871	*No Competition*				
1872	Tom Morris Jnr	166	3	David Strath	Prestwick
1873	Tom Kidd	179	1	Jamie Anderson	St Andrews
1874	Mungo Park	159	2	Tom Morris Jnr	Musselburgh
1875	Willie Park	166	2	Bob Martin	Prestwick
1876	Bob Martin	176	—	David Strath	St Andrews
	(Martin was awarded the title when Strath refused to play-off)				
1877	Jamie Anderson	160	2	Bob Pringle	Musselburgh
1878	Jamie Anderson	157	2	Bob Kirk	Prestwick
1879	Jamie Anderson	169	3	James Allan, Andrew Kirkaldy	St Andrews
1880	Bob Ferguson	162	5	Peter Paxton	Musselburgh
1881	Bob Ferguson	170	3	Jamie Anderson	Prestwick
1882	Bob Ferguson	171	3	Willie Fernie	St Andrews
1883	Willie Fernie	159	Play-off	Bob Ferguson	Musselburgh
	(Fernie won play-off 158 to 159)				
1884	Jack Simpson	160	4	David Rollan, Willie Fernie	Prestwick
1885	Bob Martin	171	1	Archie Simpson	St Andrews
1886	David Brown	157	2	Willie Campbell	Musselburgh
1887	Willie Park Jnr	161	1	Bob Martin	Prestwick
1888	Jack Burns	171	1	David Anderson Jnr, Ben Sayers	St Andrews
1889	Willie Park Jnr	155	Play-off	Andrew Kirkaldy	Musselburgh
	(Park won play-off 158 to 163)				
1890	*John Ball	164	3	Willie Fernie, Archie Simpson	Prestwick
1891	Hugh Kirkaldy	166	2	Willie Fernie, Andrew Kirkaldy	St Andrews
(From 1892 the competition was extended to 72 holes)					
1892	*Harold Hilton	305	3	*John Ball Jnr, James Kirkaldy, Sandy Herd	Muirfield
1893	Willie Auchterlonie	322	2	*Johnny Laidlay	Prestwick

YEAR	CHAMPION	SCORE	MARGIN	RUNNERS-UP	VENUE
1894	J.H. Taylor	326	5	Douglas Rolland	Sandwich
1895	J.H. Taylor	322	4	Sandy Herd	St Andrews
1896	Harry Vardon	316	Play-off	J.H. Taylor	Muirfield
				(Vardon won play-off 157 to 161)	
1897	*Harold H. Hilton	314	1	James Braid	Hoylake
1898	Harry Vardon	307	1	Willie Park	Prestwick
1899	Harry Vardon	310	5	Jack White	Sandwich
1900	J.H. Taylor	309	8	Harry Vardon	St Andrews
1901	James Braid	309	3	Harry Vardon	Muirfield
1902	Sandy Herd	307	1	Harry Vardon, James Braid	Hoylake
1903	Harry Vardon	300	6	Tom Vardon	Prestwick
1904	Jack White	296	1	James Braid, J.H. Taylor	Sandwich
1905	James Braid	318	5	J.H. Taylor, R. Jones	St Andrews
1906	James Braid	300	4	J.H. Taylor	Muirfield
1907	Arnaud Massy	312	2	J.H. Taylor	Hoylake
1908	James Braid	291	8	Tom Ball	Prestwick
1909	J.H. Taylor	295	4	James Braid	Deal
1910	James Braid	299	4	Sandy Herd	St Andrews
1911	Harry Vardon	303	Play-off	Arnaud Massy	Sandwich
				(Play-off; Massy conceded at the 35th hole)	
1912	Ted Ray	295	4	Harry Vardon	Muirfield
1913	J.H. Taylor	304	8	Ted Ray	Hoylake
1914	Harry Vardon	306	3	J.H. Taylor	Prestwick
1915-1919 No Championship					
1920	George Duncan	303	2	Sandy Herd	Deal
1921	Jock Hutchison	296	Play-off	*Roger Wethered	St Andrews
				(Hutchison won play-off 150 to 159)	
1922	Walter Hagen	300	1	George Duncan, Jim Barnes	Sandwich
1923	Arthur G. Havers	295	1	Walter Hagen	Troon
1924	Walter Hagen	301	1	Ernest Whitcombe	Hoylake
1925	Jim Barnes	300	1	Archie Compston, Ted Ray	Prestwick
1926	*Robert T. Jones Jnr	291	2	Al Watrous	Royal Lytham
1927	*Robert T. Jones Jnr	285	6	Aubrey Boomer, Fred Robson	St Andrews
1928	Walter Hagen	292	2	Gene Sarazen	Sandwich
1929	Walter Hagen	292	6	John Farrell	Muirfield
1930	*Robert T. Jones Jnr	291	2	Leo Diegel, Macdonald Smith	Hoylake
1931	Tommy Armour	296	1	Jose Jurado	Carnoustie
1932	Gene Sarazen	283	5	Macdonald Smith	Prince's
1933	Densmore Shute	292	Play-off	Craig Wood	St Andrews
				(Shute won play-off 149 to 154)	
1934	Henry Cotton	283	5	Sid Brews	Sandwich
1935	Alf Perry	283	4	Alf Padgham	Muirfield
1936	Alf Padgham	287	1	Jimmy Adams	Hoylake
1937	Henry Cotton	290	2	Reg Whitcombe	Carnoustie
1938	Reg Whitcombe	295	2	Jimmy Adams	Sandwich
1939	Richard Burton	290	2	Johnny Bulla	St Andrews
1940-1945 No Championship					
1946	Sam Snead	290	4	Bobby Locke, Johnny Bulla	St Andrews
1947	Fred Daly	293	1	Reg Horne, *Frank Stranahan	Hoylake
1948	Henry Cotton	284	5	Fred Daly	Muirfield
1949	Bobby Locke	283	Play-off	Harry Bradshaw	Sandwich
				(Locke won play-off 135 to 147)	
1950	Bobby Locke	279	2	Roberto de Vicenzo	Troon
1951	Max Faulkner	285	2	Tony Cerda	Royal Portrush
1952	Bobby Locke	287	1	Peter Thomson	Royal Lytham

YEAR	CHAMPION	SCORE	MARGIN	RUNNERS-UP	VENUE
1953	Ben Hogan	282	4	*Frank Stranahan, Dai Rees, Peter Thomson, Tony Cerda	Carnoustie
1954	Peter Thomson	283	1	Sid Scott, Dai Rees, Bobby Locke	Royal Birkdale
1955	Peter Thomson	281	2	Johnny Fallon	St Andrews
1956	Peter Thomson	286	3	Flory van Donck	Hoylake
1957	Bobby Locke	279	3	Peter Thomson	St Andrews
1958	Peter Thomson	278	Play-off	David Thomas (Thomson won play-off 139 to 143)	Royal Lytham
1959	Gary Player	284	2	Flory van Donck, Fred Bullock	Muirfield
1960	Kel Nagle	278	1	Arnold Palmer	St Andrews
1961	Arnold Palmer	284	1	Dai Rees	Royal Birkdale
1962	Arnold Palmer	276	6	Kel Nagle	Troon
1963	Bob Charles	277	Play-off	Phil Rodgers (Charles won play-off 140 to 148)	Royal Lytham
1964	Tony Lema	279	5	Jack Nicklaus	St Andrews
1965	Peter Thomson	285	2	Christy O'Connor, Brian Huggett	Royal Birkdale
1966	Jack Nicklaus	282	1	David Thomas, Doug Sanders	Muirfield
1967	Roberto de Vicenzo	278	2	Jack Nicklaus	Hoylake
1968	Gary Player	289	2	Jack Nicklaus, Bob Charles	Carnoustie
1969	Tony Jacklin	280	2	Bob Charles	Royal Lytham
1970	Jack Nicklaus	283	Play-off	Doug Sanders (Nicklaus won play-off 72 to 73)	St Andrews
1971	Lee Trevino	278	1	Lu Liang Huan	Royal Birkdale
1972	Lee Trevino	278	1	Jack Nicklaus	Muirfield
1973	Tom Weiskopf	276	3	Neil Coles, Johnny Miller	Troon
1974	Gary Player	282	4	Peter Oosterhuis	Royal Lytham
1975	Tom Watson	279	Play-off	Jack Newton (Watson won play-off 71 to 72)	Carnoustie
1976	Johnny Miller	279	6	Jack Nicklaus, Severiano Ballesteros	Royal Birkdale
1977	Tom Watson	268	1	Jack Nicklaus	Turnberry
1978	Jack Nicklaus	281	2	Simon Owen, Ben Crenshaw, Raymond Floyd, Tom Kite	St Andrews
1979	Severiano Ballesteros	283	3	Jack Nicklaus, Ben Crenshaw	Royal Lytham
1980	Tom Watson	271	4	Lee Trevino	Muirfield
1981	Bill Rogers	276	4	Bernhard Langer	Sandwich
1982	Tom Watson	284	1	Peter Oosterhuis, Nick Price	Troon
1983	Tom Watson	275	1	Hale Irwin, Andy Bean	Royal Birkdale
1984	Severiano Ballesteros	276	2	Bernhard Langer, Tom Watson	St Andrews
1985	Sandy Lyle	282	1	Payne Stewart	Sandwich
1986	Greg Norman	280	5	Gordon J. Brand	Turnberry
1987	Nick Faldo	279	1	Rodger Davis, Paul Azinger	Muirfield
1988	Severiano Ballesteros	273	2	Nick Price	Royal Lytham
1989	Mark Calcavecchia	275	Play-off	Greg Norman, Wayne Grady (Calcavecchia won four-hole play-off)	Royal Troon
1990	Nick Faldo	270	5	Mark McNulty, Payne Stewart	St Andrews
1991	Ian Baker-Finch	272	2	Mike Harwood	Royal Birkdale
1992	Nick Faldo	272	1	John Cook	Muirfield
1993	Greg Norman	267	2	Nick Faldo	Sandwich
1994	Nick Price	268	1	Jesper Parnevik	Turnberry
1995	John Daly	282	Play-off	Costantino Rocca (Daly won four-hole play-off)	St Andrews
1996	Tom Lehman	271	2	Mark McCumber, Ernie Els	Royal Lytham
1997	Justin Leonard	272	3	Jesper Parnevik, Darren Clarke	Royal Troon
1998	Mark O'Meara	280	Play-off	Brian Watts (O'Meara won four-hole play-off)	Royal Birkdale

*Denotes amateurs

Tom Watson (1975, 1977, 1980, 1982, 1983)

Sandy Lyle (1985)

Mark Calcavecchia (1989)

Nick Price (1994)

Gary Player (1959, 1968, 1974)

OPEN CHAMPIONSHIP

MOST VICTORIES
6, Harry Vardon, 1896-98-99-1903-11-14
5, James Braid, 1901-05-06-08-10; J.H. Taylor, 1894-95-1900-09-13; Peter Thomson, 1954-55-56-58-65; Tom Watson, 1975-77-80-82-83

MOST TIMES RUNNER-UP OR JOINT RUNNER-UP
7, Jack Nicklaus, 1964-67-68-72-76-77-79
6, J.H. Taylor, 1896-1904-05-06-07-14

OLDEST WINNER
Old Tom Morris, 46 years 99 days, 1867
Roberto de Vicenzo, 44 years 93 days, 1967

YOUNGEST WINNER
Young Tom Morris, 17 years 5 months 8 days, 1868
Willie Auchterlonie, 21 years 24 days, 1893
Severiano Ballesteros, 22 years 3 months 12 days, 1979

YOUNGEST AND OLDEST COMPETITOR
Young Tom Morris, 14 years 4 months 4 days, 1865
Gene Sarazen, 71 years 4 months 13 days, 1973

BIGGEST MARGIN OF VICTORY
13 strokes, Old Tom Morris, 1862
12 strokes, Young Tom Morris, 1870
8 strokes, J.H. Taylor, 1900 and 1913; James Braid, 1908
6 strokes, Bobby Jones, 1927; Walter Hagen, 1929; Arnold Palmer, 1962; Johnny Miller, 1976

LOWEST WINNING AGGREGATES
267 (66, 68, 69, 64), Greg Norman, Royal St George's, 1993
268 (68, 70, 65, 65), Tom Watson, Turnberry, 1977; (69, 66, 67, 66), Nick Price, Turnberry, 1994
270 (67, 65, 67, 71), Nick Faldo, St Andrews, 1990

LOWEST AGGREGATES BY RUNNER-UP
269 (68, 70, 65, 66), Jack Nicklaus, Turnberry, 1977; (69, 63, 70, 67), Nick Faldo, Royal St George's, 1993; (68, 66, 68, 67), Jesper Parnevik, Turnberry, 1994

LOWEST AGGREGATE BY AN AMATEUR
281 (68, 72, 70, 71), Iain Pyman, Royal St George's, 1993; (75, 66, 70, 70), Tiger Woods, Royal Lytham, 1996

LOWEST INDIVIDUAL ROUND
63, Mark Hayes, second round, Turnberry, 1977; Isao Aoki, third round, Muirfield, 1980; Greg Norman, second round, Turnberry, 1986; Paul Broadhurst, third round, St Andrews, 1990; Jodie Mudd, fourth round, Royal Birkdale, 1991; Nick Faldo, second round, and Payne Stewart, fourth round, Royal St George's, 1993

LOWEST INDIVIDUAL ROUND BY AN AMATEUR
66, Frank Stranahan, fourth round, Troon, 1950; Tiger Woods, second round, Royal Lytham, 1996; Justin Rose, second round, Royal Birkdale, 1998

LOWEST FIRST ROUND
64, Craig Stadler, Royal Birkdale, 1983; Christy O'Connor Jr., Royal St George's, 1985; Rodger Davis, Muirfield, 1987; Raymond Floyd and Steve Pate, Muirfield, 1992

LOWEST SECOND ROUND
63, Mark Hayes, Turnberry, 1977; Greg Norman, Turnberry, 1986; Nick Faldo, Royal St George's, 1993

LOWEST THIRD ROUND
63, Isao Aoki, Muirfield, 1980; Paul Broadhurst, St Andrews, 1990

LOWEST FOURTH ROUND
63, Jodie Mudd, Royal Birkdale, 1991; Payne Stewart, Royal St George's, 1993

LOWEST FIRST 36 HOLES
130 (66, 64), Nick Faldo, Muirfield, 1992

LOWEST SECOND 36 HOLES
130 (65, 65), Tom Watson, Turnberry, 1977; (64, 66), Ian Baker-Finch, Royal Birkdale, 1991; (66, 64), Anders Forsbrand, Turnberry, 1994

LOWEST FIRST 54 HOLES
198 (67, 67, 64), Tom Lehman, Royal Lytham, 1996

LOWEST FINAL 54 HOLES
199 (66, 67, 66), Nick Price, Turnberry, 1994

LOWEST 9 HOLES
28, Denis Durnian, first 9, Royal Birkdale, 1983
29, Peter Thomson and Tom Haliburton, first 9, Royal

Lytham, 1958; Tony Jacklin, first 9, St Andrews, 1970; Bill Longmuir, first 9, Royal Lytham, 1979; David J. Russell, first 9, Royal Lytham, 1988; Ian Baker-Finch and Paul Broadhurst, first 9, St Andrews, 1990; Ian Baker-Finch, first 9, Royal Birkdale, 1991; Paul McGinley, first 9, Royal Lytham, 1996

CHAMPIONS IN THREE DECADES
Harry Vardon, 1896, 1903, 1911
J.H. Taylor, 1894, 1900, 1913
Gary Player, 1959, 1968, 1974

BIGGEST SPAN BETWEEN FIRST AND LAST VICTORIES
19 years, J.H. Taylor, 1894-1913
18 years, Harry Vardon, 1896-1914
15 years, Gary Player, 1959-74
14 years, Henry Cotton, 1934-48

SUCCESSIVE VICTORIES
4, Young Tom Morris, 1868-72. No championship in 1871
3, Jamie Anderson, 1877-79; Bob Ferguson, 1880-82, Peter Thomson, 1954-56
2, Old Tom Morris, 1861-62; J.H. Taylor, 1894-95; Harry Vardon, 1898-99; James Braid, 1905-06; Bobby Jones, 1926-27; Walter Hagen, 1928-29; Bobby Locke, 1949-50; Arnold Palmer, 1961-62; Lee Trevino, 1971-72; Tom Watson, 1982-83

VICTORIES BY AMATEURS
3, Bobby Jones, 1926-27-30
2, Harold Hilton, 1892-97
1, John Ball, 1890
Roger Wethered lost a play-off in 1921

HIGHEST NUMBER OF TOP FIVE FINISHES
16, J.H. Taylor, Jack Nicklaus
15, Harry Vardon, James Braid

HIGHEST NUMBER OF ROUNDS UNDER 70
33, Jack Nicklaus, Nick Faldo
27, Tom Watson
23, Greg Norman
21, Lee Trevino
20, Severiano Ballesteros, Nick Price

OUTRIGHT LEADER AFTER EVERY ROUND
Willie Auchterlonie, 1893; J.H. Taylor, 1894 and 1900; James Braid, 1908; Ted Ray, 1912; Bobby Jones, 1927; Gene Sarazen, 1932; Henry Cotton, 1934; Tom Weiskopf, 1973

RECORD LEADS (SINCE 1892)
After 18 holes:
4 strokes, James Braid, 1908; Bobby Jones, 1927; Henry Cotton, 1934; Christy O'Connor Jr., 1985
After 36 holes:
9 strokes, Henry Cotton, 1934
After 54 holes:
10 strokes, Henry Cotton, 1934
7 strokes, Tony Lema, 1964
6 strokes, James Braid, 1908; Tom Lehman, 1996

CHAMPIONS WITH EACH ROUND LOWER THAN PREVIOUS ONE
Jack White, 1904, Sandwich, (80, 75, 72, 69)
James Braid, 1906, Muirfield, (77, 76, 74, 73)
Ben Hogan, 1953, Carnoustie, (73, 71, 70, 68)
Gary Player, 1959, Muirfield, (75, 71, 70, 68)

CHAMPION WITH FOUR ROUNDS THE SAME
Densmore Shute, 1933, St Andrews, (73, 73, 73, 73) (excluding the play-off)

BIGGEST VARIATION BETWEEN ROUNDS OF A CHAMPION
14 strokes, Henry Cotton, 1934, second round 65, fourth round 79
11 strokes, Jack White, 1904, first round 80, fourth round 69; Greg Norman, 1986, first round 74, second round 63, third round 74

BIGGEST VARIATION BETWEEN TWO ROUNDS
18 strokes, A. Tingey Jr., 1923, first round 94, second round 76
17 strokes, Jack Nicklaus, 1981, first round 83, second round 66; Ian Baker-Finch, 1986, first round 86, second round 69

BEST COMEBACK BY CHAMPIONS
After 18 holes:
Harry Vardon, 1896, 11 strokes behind the leader
After 36 holes:
George Duncan, 1920, 13 strokes behind the leader
After 54 holes:
Jim Barnes, 1925, 5 strokes behind the leader
Tommy Armour, 1931, 5 strokes behind the leader
Justin Leonard, 1997, 5 strokes behind the leader
Of non-champions, Greg Norman, 1989, 7 strokes behind the leader and lost in a play-off

CHAMPIONS WITH FOUR ROUNDS UNDER 70
Greg Norman, 1993, Royal St George's, (66, 68, 69, 64); Nick Price, 1994, Turnberry, (69, 66, 67, 66)
Of non-champions:
Ernie Els, 1993, Royal St George's, (68, 69, 69, 68); Jesper Parnevik, 1994, Turnberry, (68, 66, 68, 67)

BEST FINISHING ROUND BY A CHAMPION
64, Greg Norman, Royal St George's, 1993
65, Tom Watson, Turnberry, 1977; Severiano Ballesteros, Royal Lytham, 1988; Justin Leonard, Royal Troon, 1997
66, Johnny Miller, Royal Birkdale, 1976; Ian Baker-Finch, Royal Birkdale, 1991; Nick Price, Turnberry, 1994

WORST FINISHING ROUND BY A CHAMPION SINCE 1920
79, Henry Cotton, Sandwich, 1934
78, Reg Whitcombe, Sandwich, 1938
77, Walter Hagen, Hoylake, 1924

WORST OPENING ROUND BY A CHAMPION SINCE 1919
80, George Duncan, Deal, 1920 (he also had a second round of 80)
77, Walter Hagen, Hoylake, 1924

BEST OPENING ROUND BY A CHAMPION

66, Peter Thomson, Royal Lytham, 1958; Nick Faldo, Muirfield, 1992; Greg Norman, Royal St George's, 1993
67, Henry Cotton, Sandwich, 1934; Tom Watson, Royal Birkdale, 1983; Severiano Ballesteros, Royal Lytham, 1988; Nick Faldo, St Andrews, 1990; John Daly, St Andrews, 1995; Tom Lehman, Royal Lytham, 1996

BIGGEST RECOVERY IN 18 HOLES BY A CHAMPION

George Duncan, Deal, 1920, was 13 strokes behind the leader, Abe Mitchell, after 36 holes and level after 54

MOST APPEARANCES ON FINAL DAY (SINCE 1892)

32, Jack Nicklaus
30, J.H. Taylor
27, Harry Vardon, James Braid
26, Peter Thomson, Gary Player
23, Dai Rees
22, Henry Cotton

CHAMPIONSHIP WITH HIGHEST NUMBER OF ROUNDS UNDER 70

148, Turnberry, 1994

CHAMPIONSHIP SINCE 1946 WITH THE FEWEST ROUNDS UNDER 70

St Andrews, 1946; Hoylake, 1947; Portrush, 1951; Hoylake, 1956; Carnoustie, 1968. All had only two rounds under 70

LONGEST COURSE

Carnoustie, 1968, 7252 yd (6631 m)

COURSES MOST OFTEN USED

St Andrews, 25; Prestwick, 24; Muirfield, 14; Sandwich, 12; Hoylake, 10; Royal Lytham, 9; Royal Birkdale, 8; Royal Troon, 7; Musselburgh, 6; Carnoustie, 5; Turnberry, 3; Deal, 2; Royal Portrush and Prince's, 1

PRIZE MONEY

Year	Total	First Prize
1860	nil	nil
1863	10	nil
1864	16	6
1876	27	10
1889	22	8
1891	28.50	10
1892	110	(Amateur winner)
1893	100	30
1910	125	50
1920	225	75
1927	275	100
1930	400	100
1931	500	100
1946	1,000	150
1949	1,700	300
1953	2,450	500
1954	3,500	750
1955	3,750	1,000
1958	4,850	1,000
1959	5,000	1,000
1960	7,000	1,250
1961	8,500	1,400
1963	8,500	1,500
1965	10,000	1,750
1966	15,000	2,100
1968	20,000	3,000
1969	30,000	4,250
1970	40,000	5,250
1971	45,000	5,500
1972	50,000	5,500
1975	75,000	7,500
1977	100,000	10,000
1978	125,000	12,500
1979	155,000	15,500
1980	200,000	25,000
1982	250,000	32,000
1983	300,000	40,000
1984	451,000	55,000
1985	530,000	65,000
1986	600,000	70,000
1987	650,000	75,000
1988	700,000	80,000
1989	750,000	80,000
1990	825,000	85,000
1991	900,000	90,000
1992	950,000	95,000
1993	1,000,000	100,000
1994	1,100,000	110,000
1995	1,250,000	125,000
1996	1,400,000	200,000
1997	1,600,000	250,000
1998	1,800,000	300,000

ATTENDANCE

Year	Attendance
1962	37,098
1963	24,585
1964	35,954
1965	32,927
1966	40,182
1967	29,880
1968	51,819
1969	46,001
1970	81,593
1971	70,076
1972	84,746
1973	78,810
1974	92,796
1975	85,258
1976	92,021
1977	87,615
1978	125,271
1979	134,501
1980	131,610
1981	111,987
1982	133,299
1983	142,892
1984	193,126
1985	141,619
1986	134,261
1987	139,189
1988	191,334
1989	160,639
1990	208,680
1991	189,435
1992	146,427
1993	141,000
1994	128,000
1995	180,000
1996	171,000
1997	176,000
1998	195,100

COMPLETE SCORES

127TH OPEN CHAMPIONSHIP

*Denotes amateurs

HOLE		1	2	3	4	5	6	7	8	9	10	11	12	13	14	15	16	17	18	
PAR		4	4	4	3	4	4	3	4	4	4	4	3	4	3	5	4	5	4	TOTAL
Mark O'Meara	Round 1	4	4	4	3	4	4	4	4	4	4	4	3	6	3	5	3	4	5	72
USA	Round 2	4	3	5	3	4	4	3	4	4	4	4	2	4	3	5	5	3	4	68
£300,000	Round 3	6	4	4	3	5	5	3	4	4	4	4	3	3	3	5	4	4	4	72
	Round 4	4	4	4	2	4	5	4	3	4	4	3	2	5	2	5	5	4	4	68-280
	Play-off															4	4	5	4	17
Brian Watts	Round 1	5	4	3	3	4	4	3	5	5	3	3	3	4	3	4	4	4	4	68
USA	Round 2	5	3	3	5	4	5	2	4	4	4	4	2	4	3	5	4	4	4	69
£188,000	Round 3	5	4	4	3	4	5	4	4	4	4	5	4	3	3	5	4	4	4	73
	Round 4	4	4	4	4	3	4	3	4	4	4	4	4	4	3	5	4	4	4	70-280
	Play-off															5	4	5	5	19
Tiger Woods	Round 1	4	4	3	3	3	4	2	4	3	4	4	4	3	4	4	4	4	5	65
USA	Round 2	5	5	4	3	4	5	3	4	5	4	3	4	3	6	4	4	4	3	73
£135,000	Round 3	4	4	4	4	5	6	3	4	4	5	5	4	4	4	4	5	4	4	77
	Round 4	5	3	4	2	4	5	3	3	4	4	3	4	3	4	4	4	4	3	66-281
Raymond Russell	Round 1	4	4	4	3	4	5	4	3	4	4	4	3	4	3	4	3	4	4	68
Scotland	Round 2	4	5	4	4	4	4	3	4	4	4	4	3	5	3	5	5	4	4	73
£76,667	Round 3	4	5	4	3	4	4	3	4	5	5	4	3	4	3	6	4	5	5	75
	Round 4	4	4	3	3	4	4	3	4	4	4	4	3	4	2	4	4	4	4	66-282
***Justin Rose**	Round 1	4	4	5	4	4	4	3	3	4	4	3	5	3	5	4	4	4	5	72
England	Round 2	4	4	5	2	3	5	3	4	4	4	3	4	2	5	5	3	3		66
Silver Medal	Round 3	5	5	4	3	4	4	3	4	4	5	4	3	5	4	4	4	5	5	75
	Round 4	5	4	4	2	4	4	4	5	4	4	4	2	4	3	4	4	5	3	69-282
Jim Furyk	Round 1	5	4	5	3	4	4	2	4	4	4	4	3	4	3	4	4	5	4	70
USA	Round 2	4	4	3	4	3	5	3	4	4	4	4	3	4	4	5	4	4	4	70
£76,667	Round 3	4	5	3	3	5	6	3	4	4	4	4	3	4	3	5	4	4	4	72
	Round 4	4	4	4	4	3	4	4	4	4	4	2	4	3	6	4	5	4		70-282
Jesper Parnevik	Round 1	3	4	4	3	4	4	4	3	3	4	4	3	4	3	5	4	5	4	68
Sweden	Round 2	3	4	5	3	4	5	3	4	5	4	4	3	3	4	5	4	5	4	72
£76,667	Round 3	4	4	4	2	4	5	4	4	4	4	4	3	4	3	5	5	4	5	72
	Round 4	4	4	4	3	4	5	2	5	3	4	4	3	5	3	5	4	4	4	70-282
Davis Love III	Round 1	4	4	3	3	4	4	4	4	4	4	4	3	3	3	4	3	5	4	67
USA	Round 2	4	3	5	3	5	4	3	4	4	4	6	3	4	3	5	5	4	4	73
£49,500	Round 3	5	5	4	3	4	6	4	4	4	4	5	3	5	4	5	4	4	4	77
	Round 4	3	3	4	3	5	4	4	4	4	3	4	4	3	3	4	4	5	4	68-285

HOLE		1	2	3	4	5	6	7	8	9	10	11	12	13	14	15	16	17	18	
PAR		4	4	4	3	4	4	3	4	4	4	4	3	4	3	5	4	5	4	TOTAL
Costantino Rocca	Round 1	6	4	3	2	3	4	3	4	4	4	6	3	3	3	5	5	4	6	72
Italy	Round 2	5	3	4	3	4	4	4	5	4	4	4	3	4	3	8	4	4	4	74
£40,850	Round 3	4	4	3	4	4	4	3	4	4	4	4	4	4	3	5	4	4	4	70
	Round 4	5	4	3	3	5	4	3	4	4	4	4	3	4	3	4	3	6	4	70-286
Thomas Bjorn	Round 1	4	4	4	3	3	5	3	3	4	4	3	3	4	4	4	4	5	4	68
Denmark	Round 2	5	4	3	3	4	4	3	4	4	4	5	3	5	3	5	4	4	4	71
£40,850	Round 3	4	4	4	3	3	5	3	4	5	5	4	3	5	3	7	4	5	5	76
	Round 4	4	4	5	4	4	4	3	4	4	3	4	3	4	3	5	4	5	4	71-286
David Duval	Round 1	5	4	4	3	4	4	3	4	4	4	5	3	4	3	4	4	4	4	70
USA	Round 2	4	4	4	4	4	4	3	4	4	4	4	3	4	3	4	5	4	5	71
£33,333	Round 3	5	5	3	2	5	5	4	4	5	5	4	3	4	3	6	4	4	4	75
	Round 4	4	4	4	3	4	5	3	4	4	5	3	3	4	4	5	4	4	4	71-287
Brad Faxon	Round 1	5	4	3	3	4	4	3	3	3	4	5	2	5	3	5	3	4	4	67
USA	Round 2	5	4	4	4	3	5	3	4	4	5	5	2	4	4	5	5	4	4	74
£33,333	Round 3	5	4	4	4	4	5	3	4	4	4	5	3	4	3	5	5	4	5	74
	Round 4	4	4	4	3	4	5	4	5	4	3	5	3	4	3	5	3	5	4	72-287
John Huston	Round 1	4	4	4	3	4	4	3	4	4	3	3	2	4	4	5	4	3	3	65
USA	Round 2	5	4	4	2	6	4	3	4	5	5	4	3	5	4	5	5	5	4	77
£33,333	Round 3	4	4	4	3	5	4	3	4	4	4	5	3	5	3	5	5	4	4	73
	Round 4	5	4	4	3	3	4	5	3	4	4	3	3	5	3	7	3	5	4	72-287
Gordon Brand Jnr	Round 1	4	4	4	3	4	4	3	4	4	4	3	3	5	3	4	5	5	5	71
Scotland	Round 2	4	4	3	3	4	5	3	5	4	4	4	3	3	3	4	4	5	5	70
£29,000	Round 3	5	5	5	3	4	5	3	4	4	5	4	3	5	3	5	5	4	4	76
	Round 4	4	4	3	3	4	4	3	5	3	3	4	3	5	4	7	4	4	4	71-288
Jose Maria Olazabal	Round 1	4	5	4	3	5	5	3	4	4	4	3	3	4	3	6	4	5	4	73
Spain	Round 2	5	3	5	2	4	4	4	5	4	3	6	3	4	3	4	5	4	4	72
£23,650	Round 3	3	4	4	3	4	5	3	5	5	3	5	3	4	3	6	5	4	6	75
	Round 4	4	3	4	3	4	5	2	4	5	4	4	3	5	3	5	3	5	3	69-289
Peter Baker	Round 1	4	4	4	4	4	4	3	3	3	4	4	3	5	3	5	4	4	4	69
England	Round 2	4	4	4	3	3	5	3	4	5	4	5	3	4	4	5	4	4	4	72
£23,650	Round 3	5	7	4	4	4	5	3	4	4	4	5	2	6	3	5	4	4	4	77
	Round 4	4	5	4	3	4	3	3	4	4	4	4	3	4	3	5	4	5	5	71-289
Des Smyth	Round 1	4	4	5	3	4	5	3	4	4	4	4	3	5	3	5	4	5	5	74
Ireland	Round 2	4	4	4	3	4	4	3	4	4	4	3	3	4	3	5	4	4	4	69
£23,650	Round 3	4	4	4	3	4	5	4	4	5	5	4	3	4	4	5	4	5	4	75
	Round 4	5	4	4	3	5	3	3	5	5	3	4	3	4	3	4	4	5	4	71-289
Greg Turner	Round 1	4	4	4	3	4	5	2	4	3	4	5	3	4	3	4	3	4	5	68
New Zealand	Round 2	5	4	4	3	5	4	3	4	5	4	4	4	4	3	5	5	4	5	75
£23,650	Round 3	4	6	3	3	4	5	3	5	4	5	4	3	4	4	5	4	4	5	75
	Round 4	4	3	4	3	4	5	3	5	4	4	4	4	4	3	4	4	5	4	71-289
Robert Allenby	Round 1	4	4	4	3	4	3	2	4	4	4	4	3	4	3	5	4	4	4	67
Australia	Round 2	4	5	4	4	4	5	3	5	6	3	6	3	5	3	5	3	4	4	76
£17,220	Round 3	4	5	4	4	4	4	4	4	4	4	5	3	5	3	6	6	5	4	78
	Round 4	4	4	4	3	4	4	2	4	5	3	5	3	5	4	4	4	4	3	69-290
Curtis Strange	Round 1	5	3	5	3	4	5	3	4	4	4	5	3	4	4	4	4	4	5	73
USA	Round 2	4	4	4	3	4	5	3	5	4	4	4	4	3	5	4	5	4	4	73
£17,220	Round 3	5	5	4	3	4	5	2	4	3	5	5	3	4	4	5	5	4	4	74
	Round 4	4	4	4	2	3	4	3	4	3	5	5	3	4	4	5	4	5	4	70-290

HOLE		1	2	3	4	5	6	7	8	9	10	11	12	13	14	15	16	17	18	
PAR		4	4	4	3	4	4	3	4	4	4	4	3	4	3	5	4	5	4	TOTAL
Vijay Singh	Round 1	4	3	3	3	4	4	3	4	4	4	4	3	4	3	5	4	3	5	67
Fiji	Round 2	5	5	3	3	5	4	4	4	4	3	4	4	4	4	5	5	4	4	74
£17,220	Round 3	5	5	4	2	5	5	4	4	5	5	4	3	5	3	5	5	5	4	78
	Round 4	3	5	5	3	4	4	3	5	4	5	4	3	4	3	4	4	5	3	71-290
Mark James	Round 1	5	3	4	3	4	3	3	4	4	4	4	3	5	3	5	4	5	5	71
England	Round 2	5	5	4	3	5	5	2	5	4	4	4	3	6	3	6	4	3	3	74
£17,220	Round 3	6	6	4	4	4	4	2	4	5	3	5	3	4	2	5	6	4	3	74
	Round 4	3	4	4	3	4	6	3	3	4	4	4	3	6	3	4	4	5	4	71-290
Sandy Lyle	Round 1	4	4	4	3	4	4	3	4	6	4	4	4	4	3	4	4	4	4	71
Scotland	Round 2	3	4	4	3	4	4	3	4	5	3	6	3	5	3	5	5	4	4	72
£17,220	Round 3	5	4	5	2	4	4	4	4	4	4	4	4	4	5	5	4	5	4	75
	Round 4	3	5	5	3	4	4	3	4	5	4	5	3	4	4	5	3	4	4	72-290
Lee Janzen	Round 1	5	4	4	3	4	5	3	4	5	4	4	3	3	4	6	3	4	4	72
USA	Round 2	6	4	4	3	4	4	3	4	3	4	4	3	4	2	5	4	4	4	69
£12,480	Round 3	6	6	5	3	4	6	3	4	4	4	5	3	4	2	5	6	4	6	80
	Round 4	3	4	4	3	4	5	2	4	3	4	5	4	4	3	4	5	5	4	70-291
Sam Torrance	Round 1	3	4	4	2	3	4	3	4	4	4	6	3	4	3	5	4	5	4	69
Scotland	Round 2	5	5	5	3	4	5	2	4	5	4	5	4	4	3	5	5	5	4	77
£12,480	Round 3	4	5	4	3	4	5	3	4	4	5	5	3	5	4	5	4	4	4	75
	Round 4	4	4	4	3	4	4	3	4	4	4	3	4	4	3	5	4	4	5	70-291
Peter O'Malley	Round 1	4	4	4	4	3	3	2	4	4	4	5	3	5	3	4	4	6	5	71
Australia	Round 2	5	4	3	3	6	4	4	4	4	4	4	3	4	4	4	4	4	3	71
£12,480	Round 3	4	5	4	3	5	4	4	5	4	5	6	3	6	2	5	5	4	4	78
	Round 4	4	4	4	3	3	5	3	4	4	4	4	3	5	3	5	4	5	4	71-291
Stephen Ames	Round 1	5	4	3	3	4	4	3	4	3	4	4	3	3	4	4	4	5	4	68
Trinidad & Tobago	Round 2	4	5	4	3	4	5	3	4	4	4	5	4	3	4	6	4	3	3	72
£12,480	Round 3	5	5	5	4	4	4	4	4	5	4	4	4	3	5	4	5	5	5	79
	Round 4	5	4	5	3	4	4	3	4	5	4	3	4	3	3	5	4	4	5	72-291
Bob Estes	Round 1	4	4	4	2	3	4	3	4	4	4	5	5	5	3	5	4	5	4	72
USA	Round 2	4	4	4	3	5	4	4	4	4	4	4	3	3	3	4	5	4	4	70
£12,480	Round 3	5	4	4	3	4	5	3	4	5	5	4	3	4	3	5	5	6	4	76
	Round 4	5	4	4	4	4	5	3	5	4	4	3	3	3	4	6	4	4	4	73-291
Scott Dunlap	Round 1	5	4	4	2	4	4	3	4	5	4	3	4	3	5	4	4	4	6	72
USA	Round 2	4	5	4	3	3	4	4	3	4	4	4	4	4	2	5	4	4	4	69
£10,030	Round 3	6	5	4	4	5	4	4	4	4	5	4	3	3	2	7	5	6	5	80
	Round 4	5	4	4	2	4	3	3	4	5	4	4	4	3	5	4	5	4		71-292
Nick Price	Round 1	5	4	3	3	3	4	3	3	4	5	4	2	4	3	4	4	4	4	66
Zimbabwe	Round 2	4	4	4	3	4	5	3	4	5	5	4	3	4	3	5	5	3	4	72
£10,030	Round 3	5	4	4	3	4	5	3	4	5	6	5	5	5	4	5	5	5	5	82
	Round 4	4	4	4	3	4	4	3	6	4	3	4	3	5	3	5	4	5	4	72-292
***Sergio Garcia**	Round 1	4	4	3	3	4	5	3	4	3	5	4	3	4	2	4	4	5	5	69
Spain	Round 2	5	4	4	5	4	5	3	4	4	5	4	3	4	3	5	4	5	4	75
	Round 3	4	5	4	4	4	5	3	5	4	5	4	3	5	3	6	4	4	4	76
	Round 4	4	5	4	3	4	4	2	4	3	5	5	3	5	3	6	4	4	4	72-292
Ernie Els	Round 1	4	4	4	4	3	6	4	4	4	3	3	3	4	3	5	4	5	5	72
South Africa	Round 2	6	4	4	3	5	4	3	4	4	4	4	4	3	3	5	5	5	5	74
£10,030	Round 3	4	4	4	3	5	4	4	4	4	4	5	3	4	3	5	4	5	5	74
	Round 4	3	4	5	3	4	4	4	4	3	4	3	4	6	2	5	4	5	5	72-292

HOLE		1	2	3	4	5	6	7	8	9	10	11	12	13	14	15	16	17	18	
PAR		4	4	4	3	4	4	3	4	4	4	4	3	4	3	5	4	5	4	TOTAL
Loren Roberts	Round 1	4	3	3	3	4	4	3	5	4	4	4	2	4	3	4	4	4	4	66
USA	Round 2	5	5	4	3	4	5	3	4	4	5	4	4	4	3	5	5	4	5	76
£10,030	Round 3	5	5	4	3	5	5	4	4	4	4	4	3	4	4	5	5	4	4	76
	Round 4	5	4	5	3	4	4	3	4	4	3	4	5	6	3	4	4	5	4	74-292
Shigeki Maruyama	Round 1	4	4	4	2	5	4	3	4	4	4	4	3	5	4	4	4	4	4	70
Japan	Round 2	4	4	4	2	5	5	3	4	4	4	5	3	4	3	6	4	5	4	73
£10,030	Round 3	4	4	4	3	5	4	4	4	4	4	5	3	6	2	5	4	5	5	75
	Round 4	4	4	4	2	5	7	3	4	3	4	4	4	5	3	5	4	4	5	74-292
Sven Struver	Round 1	5	5	4	4	5	4	3	5	4	4	4	2	4	3	6	5	4	4	75
Germany	Round 2	4	5	3	3	3	5	3	4	5	4	4	4	4	3	5	4	3	4	70
£8,900	Round 3	5	5	4	5	4	5	3	5	5	3	6	3	4	3	5	6	5	4	80
	Round 4	3	4	5	2	4	4	4	4	3	4	3	2	5	3	4	5	5	4	68-293
Santiago Luna	Round 1	5	4	4	3	4	3	3	4	3	5	5	2	4	3	4	4	5	5	70
Spain	Round 2	5	4	5	3	5	5	3	4	5	4	4	3	3	3	4	4	4	4	72
£8,900	Round 3	5	4	5	3	5	5	4	4	5	5	4	3	4	3	5	5	6	5	80
	Round 4	5	4	3	4	4	4	3	5	4	3	3	4	4	3	6	3	5	4	71-293
Mark Calcavecchia	Round 1	4	4	4	3	4	4	3	4	3	6	3	3	4	3	5	4	4	4	69
USA	Round 2	4	4	4	3	5	5	3	5	4	7	4	3	4	4	6	4	4	4	77
£8,900	Round 3	5	5	4	3	4	4	4	3	4	3	5	3	4	3	6	5	4	4	73
	Round 4	5	4	4	3	4	5	4	4	4	4	6	3	3	3	4	4	6	4	74-293
Joakim Haeggman	Round 1	4	4	3	3	4	4	3	4	5	4	4	4	5	3	5	4	4	4	71
Sweden	Round 2	5	4	4	3	3	4	4	4	5	4	4	3	5	3	6	4	5	4	74
£8,350	Round 3	5	5	4	2	4	5	5	4	5	5	6	2	4	4	5	5	4	4	78
	Round 4	4	5	4	4	3	5	3	4	4	4	5	3	5	3	5	3	4	3	71-294
Steen Tinning	Round 1	5	4	5	3	4	3	3	4	4	4	3	3	4	3	4	4	5	4	69
Denmark	Round 2	5	4	4	4	4	5	4	4	5	4	5	3	4	3	5	5	4	4	76
£8,350	Round 3	4	5	4	3	3	4	4	4	4	4	4	5	4	3	7	5	5	5	77
	Round 4	5	3	5	3	3	5	3	4	4	4	4	3	5	3	5	4	5	4	72-294
Patrik Sjoland	Round 1	5	5	5	3	4	4	3	4	4	4	4	2	5	3	4	4	5	4	72
Sweden	Round 2	5	4	4	3	4	5	3	4	4	5	5	3	4	3	4	5	3	4	72
£8,350	Round 3	5	4	4	3	6	5	3	4	4	4	4	3	5	4	5	4	5	5	77
	Round 4	5	3	5	3	3	4	4	5	5	4	4	2	5	3	5	4	5	4	73-294
Naomichi Ozaki	Round 1	4	5	5	3	4	5	3	4	4	4	4	3	4	3	4	4	4	5	72
Japan	Round 2	5	4	4	4	4	5	3	4	4	4	4	3	4	3	5	5	4	4	73
£8,350	Round 3	4	5	4	3	6	4	3	4	4	4	5	3	4	3	5	6	4	5	76
	Round 4	4	4	4	3	4	4	3	4	4	4	5	5	5	3	4	5	4	4	73-294
Tom Kite	Round 1	6	4	4	3	4	4	3	4	4	3	4	3	4	3	5	4	5	5	72
USA	Round 2	5	3	4	3	4	4	3	4	4	3	4	3	5	3	5	4	5	3	69
£8,350	Round 3	5	5	4	3	4	5	3	4	5	4	4	4	5	5	5	4	5	5	79
	Round 4	4	4	3	2	4	4	3	5	3	4	4	4	6	3	5	6	5	5	74-294
Philip Walton	Round 1	3	5	3	2	4	4	3	4	4	5	5	2	4	3	4	4	4	5	68
Ireland	Round 2	4	5	4	3	4	5	3	4	4	3	4	3	5	3	5	6	7	4	76
£8,350	Round 3	5	5	3	3	4	5	3	4	4	4	4	2	4	4	5	6	5	4	74
	Round 4	4	4	4	4	4	5	3	5	3	5	4	3	4	4	6	4	5	5	76-294
David Howell	Round 1	4	5	4	3	4	4	3	4	4	5	3	2	5	2	3	4	4	5	68
England	Round 2	3	4	4	3	4	3	4	5	5	5	4	3	5	4	7	4	5	5	77
£7,581	Round 3	6	4	4	3	5	5	4	5	4	4	5	4	5	4	5	3	5	4	79
	Round 4	3	4	4	3	4	5	3	5	4	4	4	3	5	3	5	4	4	4	71-295

HOLE		1	2	3	4	5	6	7	8	9	10	11	12	13	14	15	16	17	18	
PAR		4	4	4	3	4	4	3	4	4	4	4	3	4	3	5	4	5	4	TOTAL
Rodger Davis	Round 1	4	4	5	2	4	6	4	4	4	4	6	2	4	3	5	6	5	4	76
Australia	Round 2	5	4	4	3	3	5	3	4	4	4	4	3	4	3	5	4	4	4	70
£7,581	Round 3	4	5	5	4	4	5	3	4	5	3	6	3	5	4	6	4	4	4	78
	Round 4	5	4	5	3	4	4	2	4	4	3	3	2	5	4	5	5	5	4	71-295
David Frost	Round 1	5	5	4	3	4	5	2	3	4	4	4	3	4	3	4	4	6	5	72
South Africa	Round 2	5	4	3	3	5	4	3	4	4	3	4	3	4	3	5	7	5	4	73
£7,581	Round 3	4	4	5	4	5	4	4	4	4	5	4	3	4	5	6	5	4	4	78
	Round 4	4	4	4	3	4	3	3	5	5	4	4	3	6	2	5	4	5	4	72-295
David Carter	Round 1	4	3	4	3	4	5	3	3	5	4	4	3	4	3	5	5	5	4	71
England	Round 2	5	3	4	3	4	5	3	5	4	5	4	3	4	3	7	4	5	4	75
£7,581	Round 3	4	4	3	3	6	4	4	4	4	5	4	4	4	3	6	4	4	6	76
	Round 4	4	4	5	3	4	5	3	4	4	4	5	3	5	3	4	4	5	4	73-295
Payne Stewart	Round 1	4	4	3	3	4	4	3	3	5	4	5	3	4	3	5	5	4	5	71
USA	Round 2	4	4	3	3	4	4	4	4	4	4	4	4	4	2	5	5	5	4	71
£7,581	Round 3	5	5	4	4	5	4	5	4	4	5	5	4	4	2	5	4	5	4	78
	Round 4	4	4	5	5	4	4	3	4	4	4	3	4	5	4	4	5	6	3	75-295
Nick Faldo	Round 1	4	4	4	2	4	4	4	3	5	4	4	3	5	4	5	4	5	4	72
England	Round 2	5	3	4	4	4	5	3	4	4	4	4	3	5	3	6	4	4	4	73
£7,581	Round 3	5	5	4	2	5	5	3	4	4	4	4	3	3	6	5	5	4	5	75
	Round 4	5	4	4	4	4	5	3	5	4	4	4	4	3	3	5	4	5	4	75-295
Andrew Coltart	Round 1	4	4	4	3	4	5	2	4	4	5	4	3	4	3	3	3	5	4	68
Scotland	Round 2	4	5	3	4	5	5	4	4	3	5	6	3	3	3	5	6	5	4	77
£7,581	Round 3	4	5	5	2	4	5	4	4	6	3	4	3	4	4	5	5	4	4	75
	Round 4	5	4	4	3	4	5	3	6	4	4	4	3	4	3	7	4	4	4	75-295
Katsuyoshi Tomori	Round 1	5	5	4	3	5	5	4	4	3	4	4	3	3	4	5	5	5	4	75
Japan	Round 2	5	4	4	3	4	5	3	4	4	3	4	3	4	4	5	4	4	4	71
£7,581	Round 3	4	4	3	4	4	4	3	3	4	5	2	4	3	6	5	4	4	4	70
	Round 4	4	5	4	4	4	5	3	5	5	3	5	4	6	4	5	4	5	4	79-295
Brandt Jobe	Round 1	4	4	3	3	4	4	4	4	3	5	4	3	5	3	5	4	4	4	70
USA	Round 2	4	4	4	3	4	4	4	4	5	5	4	3	4	3	5	5	4	4	73
£6,860	Round 3	4	5	4	3	5	5	4	5	4	5	4	3	4	3	5	4	9	6	82
	Round 4	5	4	4	2	3	5	4	4	4	4	3	4	3	4	4	5	5	4	71-296
Larry Mize	Round 1	4	4	5	3	4	5	3	4	4	4	3	3	5	2	5	4	4	4	70
USA	Round 2	4	4	4	3	4	4	3	5	5	4	4	4	4	4	6	4	5	4	75
£6,860	Round 3	4	5	5	3	4	5	3	5	4	5	4	4	4	4	5	5	5	5	79
	Round 4	4	3	4	3	5	5	3	5	4	3	4	2	5	3	5	4	4	6	72-296
Steve Stricker	Round 1	5	4	4	3	5	5	3	4	3	4	3	4	3	4	4	4	4	4	70
USA	Round 2	4	4	4	2	5	4	3	4	5	4	4	4	4	4	5	4	4	4	72
£6,860	Round 3	3	5	4	3	5	7	4	4	4	7	4	4	4	4	5	4	5	4	80
	Round 4	5	5	4	2	4	4	3	5	4	4	5	5	4	3	4	5	4	4	74-296
Billy Mayfair	Round 1	5	4	5	2	5	6	3	4	4	4	6	2	4	3	4	4	4	3	72
USA	Round 2	3	4	4	3	4	6	3	4	4	4	3	4	4	4	6	4	6	3	73
£6,860	Round 3	4	5	5	4	5	5	4	4	5	4	3	5	3	5	5	5	3	4	77
	Round 4	4	4	4	2	4	5	3	5	4	4	4	4	3	6	4	6	4	4	74-296
Frankie Minoza	Round 1	4	4	4	3	4	4	3	5	5	3	4	2	4	3	5	4	4	4	69
Philippines	Round 2	5	3	4	2	4	5	4	4	5	6	4	3	4	3	6	5	5	3	75
£6,860	Round 3	4	5	4	5	4	4	3	5	4	5	5	3	4	3	5	4	5	4	76
	Round 4	4	4	4	3	5	4	4	4	4	4	4	5	5	3	5	4	5	5	76-296

HOLE		1	2	3	4	5	6	7	8	9	10	11	12	13	14	15	16	17	18	
PAR		4	4	4	3	4	4	3	4	4	4	4	3	4	3	5	4	5	4	TOTAL
Justin Leonard	Round 1	4	3	4	3	5	4	3	5	3	4	5	3	6	3	5	4	4	5	73
USA	Round 2	5	4	4	3	4	4	2	5	5	4	5	3	3	2	5	5	6	4	73
£6,264	Round 3	4	6	5	2	4	6	3	4	5	5	6	4	5	4	5	5	5	4	82
	Round 4	4	4	4	3	3	4	3	4	5	3	4	3	5	3	5	3	5	4	69-297
Trevor Dodds	Round 1	5	4	4	4	4	5	3	4	4	4	5	2	4	3	4	5	5	4	73
Namibia	Round 2	5	4	4	3	4	4	3	4	5	4	5	4	3	3	4	4	4	4	71
£6,264	Round 3	4	6	4	4	5	6	3	4	5	5	4	4	4	3	5	5	5	5	81
	Round 4	4	4	4	3	4	5	3	5	4	4	4	3	4	4	5	4	4	4	72-297
Ignacio Garrido	Round 1	3	4	5	2	4	4	3	4	4	4	4	3	4	3	5	4	6	5	71
Spain	Round 2	4	6	3	3	4	5	2	4	4	4	5	3	5	3	6	6	3	4	74
£6,264	Round 3	5	5	4	4	4	5	3	4	4	5	6	5	4	3	5	5	4	5	80
	Round 4	5	4	4	3	4	4	3	4	4	4	4	4	4	3	5	4	5	4	72-297
Steve Jones	Round 1	4	4	4	4	4	5	3	4	4	5	5	4	4	3	4	5	3	4	73
USA	Round 2	4	4	4	4	3	5	4	4	5	3	4	3	4	4	4	5	4	4	72
£6,264	Round 3	5	5	4	3	5	5	3	4	5	5	5	4	5	3	5	4	4	5	79
	Round 4	5	4	4	4	4	4	2	5	4	4	4	3	4	3	5	4	5	5	73-297
Greg Chalmers	Round 1	7	4	4	3	4	5	3	3	4	4	4	4	3	2	4	3	6	4	71
Australia	Round 2	5	3	3	4	4	5	4	4	5	5	4	3	4	3	5	4	4	6	75
£6,264	Round 3	5	5	4	4	3	5	3	4	5	3	5	3	4	2	7	5	6	4	77
	Round 4	5	4	4	3	4	4	3	5	4	3	4	5	4	3	5	5	5	4	74-297
Ian Woosnam	Round 1	5	4	4	3	3	5	3	4	3	4	4	3	6	3	5	4	5	4	72
Wales	Round 2	5	5	4	3	3	5	4	4	4	3	4	4	4	3	5	5	4	5	74
£6,264	Round 3	5	4	4	3	4	5	4	4	5	5	4	3	4	4	6	4	4	4	76
	Round 4	4	4	4	3	4	4	3	5	5	3	4	4	4	5	5	4	5	5	75-297
Eduardo Romero	Round 1	4	4	4	2	5	4	3	4	4	4	5	3	4	4	5	4	4	4	71
Argentina	Round 2	4	4	4	3	4	6	3	3	3	4	4	3	4	4	5	4	4	4	70
£6,264	Round 3	4	4	6	4	5	5	4	4	6	5	5	3	5	3	4	4	4	4	79
	Round 4	5	5	4	3	4	5	3	4	3	3	4	5	5	5	5	5	5	4	77-297
Lee Westwood	Round 1	5	4	4	4	4	4	3	4	4	4	4	3	4	3	6	3	4	4	71
England	Round 2	4	5	4	3	4	4	3	4	5	4	4	3	4	3	5	4	4	4	71
£5,975	Round 3	6	7	5	3	4	5	3	4	4	5	4	3	4	3	5	5	3	5	78
	Round 4	4	4	5	3	4	5	3	5	4	4	4	3	4	4	7	3	8	4	78-298
Carlos Franco	Round 1	3	4	4	3	4	4	4	4	4	4	4	3	5	4	5	5	4	3	71
Paraguay	Round 2	5	3	4	4	4	4	3	4	4	3	4	4	4	3	5	5	6	4	73
£5,975	Round 3	5	5	4	3	3	5	3	4	4	5	5	5	5	2	6	4	4	4	76
	Round 4	5	4	4	2	4	5	4	5	5	4	5	5	4	2	5	5	5	5	78-298
Stewart Cink	Round 1	4	4	4	2	4	5	2	4	3	4	4	3	6	2	5	5	5	5	71
USA	Round 2	4	4	3	3	4	5	3	5	5	4	4	3	5	4	5	4	4	4	73
£5,800	Round 3	5	5	3	3	5	5	3	4	4	6	6	3	5	5	6	6	5	4	83
	Round 4	5	4	4	3	4	4	3	5	4	4	4	3	5	2	5	4	5	4	72-299
Michael Campbell	Round 1	4	3	4	3	5	5	3	4	4	4	4	3	5	3	5	4	5	5	73
New Zealand	Round 2	3	6	4	2	4	6	2	5	4	4	4	3	4	2	5	5	5	4	73
£5,800	Round 3	4	6	3	5	5	5	4	4	4	8	4	3	5	3	5	4	4	4	80
	Round 4	4	4	4	3	4	4	4	4	4	4	4	4	5	2	5	4	5	5	73-299
*Didier de Vooght	Round 1	5	3	4	3	4	5	2	4	4	4	4	3	3	3	5	4	5	4	70
Belgium	Round 2	5	6	4	3	5	5	3	4	4	4	3	4	4	3	6	4	4	5	76
	Round 3	4	5	4	3	4	5	3	5	4	6	6	3	5	4	5	4	5	5	80
	Round 4	3	4	3	3	6	4	4	5	4	4	4	3	4	3	5	4	5	5	73-299

HOLE		1	2	3	4	5	6	7	8	9	10	11	12	13	14	15	16	17	18	
PAR		4	4	4	3	4	4	3	4	4	4	4	3	4	3	5	4	5	4	TOTAL
Michael Long	Round 1	3	4	4	3	4	4	3	4	4	4	5	4	4	3	5	4	4	4	70
New Zealand	Round 2	5	4	3	4	4	4	3	4	4	6	4	3	6	2	5	5	5	4	74
£5,800	Round 3	5	4	4	3	5	5	4	4	4	4	4	4	4	4	6	5	5	4	78
	Round 4	4	4	6	3	4	5	4	4	4	4	5	4	5	3	5	4	5	4	77-299
Mark Brooks	Round 1	4	4	4	3	4	5	3	4	3	4	4	3	5	3	5	6	3	4	71
USA	Round 2	4	5	3	3	4	4	3	4	5	4	4	3	5	3	6	4	5	4	73
£5,800	Round 3	5	3	4	3	4	5	4	4	4	5	5	3	4	4	5	4	4	5	75
	Round 4	5	3	5	4	5	4	4	5	4	5	4	3	5	4	5	4	5	6	80-299
Fred Couples	Round 1	3	4	4	3	4	4	3	4	4	4	3	3	3	4	3	4	5	4	66
USA	Round 2	5	4	4	3	4	5	3	5	5	4	4	3	5	3	5	4	5	3	74
£5,800	Round 3	6	5	4	4	5	5	3	4	5	4	4	3	4	4	5	5	5	3	78
	Round 4	5	5	4	3	4	8	3	5	4	4	4	4	5	3	4	4	7	5	81-299
Andrew Clapp	Round 1	4	4	5	3	4	6	3	4	4	4	4	3	4	2	5	5	4	4	72
England	Round 2	3	5	5	3	4	4	4	4	5	4	5	3	5	3	6	4	3	4	74
£5,650	Round 3	5	4	4	3	5	5	4	4	4	5	5	3	4	4	6	6	6	4	81
	Round 4	4	6	4	3	4	4	3	5	4	4	4	3	4	3	5	4	5	4	73-300
Gary Evans	Round 1	5	4	4	2	5	4	2	4	5	4	4	3	4	3	5	3	5	3	69
England	Round 2	5	4	4	3	5	5	3	5	4	5	4	2	4	4	6	4	3	4	74
£5,600	Round 3	6	5	4	4	4	5	4	4	5	5	4	4	5	3	5	5	6	6	84
	Round 4	4	5	4	3	4	4	3	4	5	4	5	2	4	3	6	5	5	4	74-301
Bob May	Round 1	5	5	3	3	4	3	3	4	4	4	5	3	4	3	5	3	5	4	70
USA	Round 2	4	5	4	4	5	4	3	4	5	4	4	3	4	2	5	4	5	4	73
£5,600	Round 3	8	4	5	4	8	5	3	4	4	6	5	3	4	3	5	4	6	4	85
	Round 4	5	5	4	3	4	5	3	4	5	4	4	4	5	2	5	4	5	4	75-303
Andrew McLardy	Round 1	4	4	5	3	4	4	3	4	4	4	5	3	5	3	5	4	5	3	72
South Africa	Round 2	5	4	4	3	4	4	3	4	5	4	4	2	4	4	6	6	4	4	74
£5,600	Round 3	4	4	4	3	4	4	4	4	4	4	5	4	6	3	6	6	6	5	80
	Round 4	6	4	3	5	4	4	3	6	4	4	4	3	5	5	5	4	5	4	78-304
Fredrik Jacobson	Round 1	4	4	4	3	5	4	3	5	3	4	3	2	4	3	4	5	3	4	67
Sweden	Round 2	5	4	4	3	4	8	4	4	4	5	4	3	5	3	6	4	3	5	78
£5,600	Round 3	5	5	4	3	4	5	3	5	5	4	5	3	5	5	6	5	5	4	81
	Round 4	5	4	4	3	5	4	3	4	5	4	6	3	6	3	5	5	5	5	79-305
Kazuhiko Hosokawa	Round 1	5	4	4	2	4	4	3	4	4	4	5	3	4	3	5	6	4	4	72
Japan	Round 2	5	5	4	4	4	5	3	4	5	4	3	3	4	3	4	5	4	4	73
£5,600	Round 3	5	5	3	3	5	7	5	4	4	4	5	3	5	3	6	4	5	5	81
	Round 4	3	4	4	3	6	4	4	5	5	5	4	5	5	4	6	3	5	5	80-306
Robert Giles	Round 1	4	5	4	3	5	4	3	3	4	4	4	3	5	3	5	5	3	5	72
England	Round 2	4	5	4	3	5	4	3	4	4	5	4	3	4	3	6	4	4	5	74
£5,600	Round 3	6	4	5	3	5	6	3	4	5	4	5	3	5	4	5	5	6	5	83
	Round 4	4	4	4	4	4	5	4	5	4	6	5	3	6	3	4	4	5	4	78-307
Phil Mickelson	Round 1	4	6	5	3	4	3	2	4	4	4	3	3	4	3	5	4	5	5	71
USA	Round 2	4	4	4	3	5	5	3	3	4	5	4	4	4	4	5	5	4	4	74
£5,600	Round 3	5	5	4	4	4	5	4	4	5	4	4	4	5	4	6	5	6	7	85
	Round 4	4	4	4	3	4	5	3	5	5	4	5	3	5	3	5	6	4	6	78-308
Andrew Oldcorn	Round 1	6	5	4	3	4	3	3	4	4	4	8	2	4	3	5	4	5	4	75
Scotland	Round 2	4	4	4	3	3	5	3	4	4	3	4	3	4	4	5	5	4	5	71
£5,600	Round 3	5	5	4	3	5	6	4	5	6	4	5	4	6	3	5	5	4	5	84
	Round 4	5	4	4	3	4	5	4	4	4	4	4	5	5	3	5	5	5	6	79-309

HOLE		1	2	3	4	5	6	7	8	9	10	11	12	13	14	15	16	17	18	TOTAL
PAR		4	4	4	3	4	4	3	4	4	4	4	3	4	3	5	4	5	4	TOTAL
Dudley Hart	Round 1	4	4	5	3	4	3	3	4	5	4	4	3	6	3	5	4	4	5	73
USA	Round 2	5	5	3	3	4	5	4	4	4	3	4	3	4	3	5	4	4	5	72
£5,600	Round 3	4	5	4	3	4	5	4	4	5	6	6	4	4	4	7	7	4	5	85
	Round 4	5	4	7	4	4	4	3	4	4	4	4	4	4	3	6	5	7	4	80-310

NON QUALIFIERS AFTER 36 HOLES

(Leading 10 professionals and ties receive £1,000 each, next 20 professionals and ties receive £800 each, next 20 professionals and ties receive £700 each, remainder of professionals receive £650 each.)

Player		1	2	3	4	5	6	7	8	9	10	11	12	13	14	15	16	17	18	TOTAL
Thomas Levet	Round 1	4	5	4	3	4	4	4	4	4	4	4	3	3	4	5	3	5	5	72
France	Round 2	4	5	4	2	4	7	4	4	4	4	4	4	4	4	5	4	4	4	75-147
Brian Davis	Round 1	5	4	4	3	4	5	3	4	4	4	4	3	4	3	5	5	5	3	72
England	Round 2	4	5	4	3	4	5	4	4	4	4	5	3	5	3	5	4	5	4	75-147
Jeff Maggert	Round 1	5	3	4	3	4	5	3	4	3	4	5	3	6	3	4	4	6	4	73
USA	Round 2	5	5	4	4	4	4	4	6	4	4	4	3	4	3	4	4	4	4	74-147
Philip Price	Round 1	4	4	4	3	5	4	3	4	4	4	4	3	5	3	4	4	5	5	72
Wales	Round 2	4	4	4	4	4	5	3	4	5	4	3	3	4	3	7	4	5	5	75-147
Craig Parry	Round 1	4	5	4	3	4	5	3	4	4	4	4	3	5	3	5	4	5	4	73
Australia	Round 2	4	4	4	4	4	4	3	4	4	5	5	3	4	3	5	5	5	4	74-147
Barry Lane	Round 1	5	3	4	2	4	5	3	4	5	5	3	3	5	3	5	3	5	5	72
England	Round 2	4	4	4	3	4	6	3	4	4	5	5	3	4	3	6	5	4	4	75-147
Keiichiro Fukabori	Round 1	4	4	4	2	5	4	3	4	3	4	4	3	5	3	6	4	4	4	70
Japan	Round 2	3	4	5	3	5	5	4	5	4	5	5	3	4	3	7	5	3	4	77-147
Colin Montgomerie	Round 1	4	4	3	3	4	3	4	4	4	4	4	4	4	3	5	5	5	5	73
Scotland	Round 2	5	5	4	4	4	5	3	4	5	4	4	4	4	3	5	5	3	3	74-147
Bob Tway	Round 1	4	4	3	4	4	5	3	4	3	4	3	3	4	3	4	4	4	5	68
USA	Round 2	5	4	4	3	5	6	3	5	4	4	5	3	4	6	5	4	4	5	79-147
Tony Johnstone	Round 1	5	4	4	2	4	5	3	4	5	4	4	3	5	3	5	4	5	4	73
Zimbabwe	Round 2	3	5	5	3	4	5	4	5	4	4	4	3	3	3	5	5	5	4	74-147
Paul McGinley	Round 1	4	3	3	4	4	4	3	4	4	4	4	3	5	3	4	5	7	5	72
Ireland	Round 2	6	5	4	3	4	4	4	4	5	3	5	3	4	4	5	4	4	4	75-147
Carl Suneson	Round 1	5	4	5	4	5	4	4	4	4	7	4	3	4	3	4	4	4	5	77
Spain	Round 2	4	4	4	3	4	4	3	4	4	5	4	4	4	3	4	4	4	4	70-147
Peter Mitchell	Round 1	5	4	5	3	4	5	4	4	4	4	4	3	4	4	5	4	5	5	76
England	Round 2	4	3	4	3	4	6	3	4	3	4	4	3	5	3	5	3	6	5	72-148
Joe Durant	Round 1	5	4	4	4	4	4	3	5	4	5	4	3	4	3	5	4	5	4	74
USA	Round 2	4	5	3	3	5	4	3	4	5	5	5	3	4	3	6	5	3	4	74-148
Yoshinori Mizumaki	Round 1	3	4	4	5	2	5	3	4	4	5	3	2	5	4	5	4	5	5	71
Japan	Round 2	5	4	5	4	4	5	3	4	4	4	4	3	5	3	4	6	6	4	77-148
Glen Day	Round 1	5	5	4	3	4	4	3	4	4	4	4	3	5	3	6	4	6	4	75
USA	Round 2	4	5	5	3	4	5	4	4	4	4	5	2	4	3	5	4	4	4	73-148
Peter Senior	Round 1	5	5	4	2	4	5	3	4	4	4	4	3	4	2	5	4	4	5	71
Australia	Round 2	4	4	4	3	4	4	5	5	4	5	5	4	4	3	6	5	4	4	77-148
***Simon McCarthy**	Round 1	5	4	4	3	5	4	3	3	5	4	4	4	3	4	4	4	5	4	73
England	Round 2	4	5	4	4	4	5	4	3	4	4	4	3	4	4	6	4	5	4	75-148
Severiano Ballesteros	Round 1	4	4	4	3	5	5	3	5	4	4	4	3	3	3	5	4	5	5	73
Spain	Round 2	5	3	4	4	4	5	3	4	5	5	5	3	4	3	5	5	4	4	75-148

HOLE		1	2	3	4	5	6	7	8	9	10	11	12	13	14	15	16	17	18	
PAR		4	4	4	3	4	4	3	4	4	4	4	3	4	3	5	4	5	4	TOTAL
Toru Taniguchi	Round 1	4	4	4	3	4	4	4	4	4	4	4	3	4	3	5	4	4	5	71
Japan	Round 2	4	6	4	3	4	6	3	4	5	4	4	3	4	2	6	5	5	5	77-148
Darren Clarke	Round 1	5	4	5	4	3	4	3	4	4	4	5	3	4	3	5	4	5	4	73
N. Ireland	Round 2	5	4	4	3	4	6	2	4	4	5	5	3	5	3	5	5	5	3	75-148
Bernhard Langer	Round 1	5	3	4	3	3	4	3	5	4	4	4	3	5	4	5	4	5	6	74
Germany	Round 2	5	5	4	4	4	5	3	4	5	5	4	3	4	3	5	4	3	5	75-149
Derrick Cooper	Round 1	4	5	4	4	4	4	3	4	4	5	4	4	3	3	5	4	4	4	72
England	Round 2	4	4	4	3	4	4	4	4	5	6	5	4	4	3	5	3	6	5	77-149
Paul Lawrie	Round 1	4	4	4	3	4	5	3	4	3	4	4	3	5	3	5	4	5	6	73
Scotland	Round 2	4	4	4	3	4	4	4	3	6	4	4	3	4	3	5	4	6	5	76-149
Richard Bland	Round 1	4	3	4	3	4	4	4	4	4	4	5	4	4	4	4	4	4	4	71
England	Round 2	4	4	4	5	4	4	3	5	5	5	6	4	4	3	4	4	5	5	78-149
Tom Watson	Round 1	4	4	4	3	4	4	2	6	4	3	4	3	5	3	5	5	5	5	73
USA	Round 2	5	4	4	3	5	5	3	4	5	5	5	3	4	3	5	4	5	4	76-149
J.P. Hayes	Round 1	5	3	4	3	3	5	3	3	5	4	4	3	4	3	5	4	5	4	70
USA	Round 2	7	4	4	3	5	4	3	7	4	4	5	3	4	2	5	5	5	5	79-149
Paul Azinger	Round 1	5	5	3	3	4	5	3	5	4	4	4	3	5	6	3	4	5	5	76
USA	Round 2	5	4	3	4	4	5	3	4	4	5	4	3	3	4	6	5	3	4	73-149
Padraig Harrington	Round 1	4	4	4	3	5	5	4	3	4	5	4	3	3	3	4	5	5	5	73
Ireland	Round 2	4	5	4	3	4	5	3	5	4	5	5	4	4	4	5	4	4	4	76-149
Gary Brown	Round 1	4	5	4	3	3	5	3	4	4	4	5	3	4	4	5	4	5	5	74
England	Round 2	4	5	4	3	4	5	4	5	5	4	5	3	4	3	5	4	4	4	75-149
Grant Dodd	Round 1	5	4	4	3	4	4	3	4	4	4	3	3	4	3	5	4	5	4	70
Australia	Round 2	5	5	4	4	5	5	3	4	4	4	7	3	5	3	6	4	4	4	79-149
Retief Goosen	Round 1	6	5	4	3	3	5	3	4	4	4	3	2	4	4	5	5	4	6	74
South Africa	Round 2	5	4	4	4	4	5	4	5	3	5	4	3	4	3	5	5	4	5	76-150
Tom Lehman	Round 1	5	4	3	3	4	5	3	4	3	4	4	3	5	3	5	4	4	5	71
USA	Round 2	4	5	4	4	5	5	3	5	4	5	5	3	4	4	5	5	5	4	79-150
David Shacklady	Round 1	5	4	4	3	5	5	4	4	4	5	4	4	5	3	5	4	5	3	76
England	Round 2	4	5	4	3	4	4	3	4	5	4	5	3	4	4	5	4	4	5	74-150
John Lovell	Round 1	5	4	5	2	4	4	4	3	5	4	5	3	5	3	4	4	4	4	72
England	Round 2	6	5	4	3	3	5	4	5	5	4	4	3	4	3	5	6	4	5	78-150
Jean Louis Guepy	Round 1	5	3	4	3	5	5	3	4	5	4	4	4	3	3	5	4	5	5	74
France	Round 2	5	4	4	3	4	5	4	4	5	5	3	4	4	4	6	5	4	3	76-150
*Matt Kuchar	Round 1	5	4	4	2	6	5	3	4	4	4	4	3	5	3	5	4	6	4	75
USA	Round 2	5	3	4	3	5	5	3	4	5	4	5	3	4	3	6	4	5	4	75-150
Scott Hoch	Round 1	4	4	4	3	4	4	3	4	5	4	4	3	4	3	5	5	3	5	73
USA	Round 2	4	5	4	3	4	5	3	4	4	5	5	4	3	5	6	4	4	5	77-150
Corey Pavin	Round 1	5	4	4	4	3	4	3	6	5	4	4	3	4	3	5	4	5	4	74
USA	Round 2	4	5	4	3	4	5	3	4	4	5	7	3	5	2	5	5	4	4	76-150
Per-Ulrik Johansson	Round 1	7	4	4	3	4	4	3	4	4	5	3	4	5	3	5	4	4	4	74
Sweden	Round 2	5	4	4	2	5	4	4	5	4	4	6	3	4	4	5	6	4	3	76-150
Kyoung Ju Choi	Round 1	3	4	4	3	4	5	2	4	4	4	5	3	5	4	4	4	4	4	70
Korea	Round 2	4	4	4	4	5	4	4	4	5	5	5	3	4	2	7	6	6	5	80-150
Lee Jones	Round 1	5	7	4	3	3	4	3	3	3	6	4	4	6	3	5	4	5	5	77
England	Round 2	4	4	4	3	4	5	3	4	5	4	4	4	3	5	5	4	4	4	73-150
Skip Kendall	Round 1	4	5	5	4	3	4	3	4	4	4	4	3	5	3	5	4	4	6	74
USA	Round 2	4	5	4	4	4	6	3	5	4	4	4	4	3	6	5	5	3		77-151

HOLE		1	2	3	4	5	6	7	8	9	10	11	12	13	14	15	16	17	18	
PAR		4	4	4	3	4	4	3	4	4	4	4	3	4	3	5	4	5	4	TOTAL
Stephen Leaney	Round 1	4	4	5	4	4	6	3	4	5	4	5	3	4	4	4	4	4	4	75
Australia	Round 2	4	4	4	4	4	5	3	5	4	4	5	3	4	3	6	5	3	6	76-151
John Daly	Round 1	4	4	4	3	4	5	4	5	3	5	4	3	5	3	5	3	5	4	73
USA	Round 2	5	4	4	4	3	4	4	5	4	4	4	3	4	4	5	3	4	10	78-151
Gary Player	Round 1	6	4	4	4	4	5	3	4	5	4	5	3	5	2	6	5	4	4	77
South Africa	Round 2	5	4	4	3	3	5	2	4	4	5	5	3	4	4	5	4	5	5	74-151
Matthew McGuire	Round 1	5	4	5	4	4	5	4	4	4	4	5	4	3	2	5	3	5	4	74
England	Round 2	5	3	4	3	4	5	3	4	5	6	5	3	5	4	4	6	4	4	77-151
Mark McNulty	Round 1	4	4	4	3	4	4	3	4	4	4	4	3	6	3	5	4	5	5	73
South Africa	Round 2	4	5	5	3	5	5	4	4	4	4	5	4	4	3	5	4	5	5	78-151
Fredrik Henge	Round 1	4	5	4	3	4	3	3	4	4	4	4	3	5	4	7	4	5	5	75
Sweden	Round 2	4	4	3	3	5	4	3	4	5	5	5	3	4	3	5	5	7	4	76-151
Howard Clark	Round 1	4	5	5	3	5	4	3	4	3	4	5	3	4	3	4	5	5	4	73
England	Round 2	4	4	4	4	4	4	4	4	4	7	5	3	4	4	5	5	5	5	79-152
Stephen Allan	Round 1	5	4	3	2	4	5	3	5	4	4	4	3	4	4	5	4	5	4	72
Australia	Round 2	5	5	4	4	5	4	4	4	5	4	6	6	4	3	6	3	4	4	80-152
Ross Drummond	Round 1	5	4	5	3	5	6	3	3	4	4	4	3	3	3	6	3	5	5	74
Scotland	Round 2	5	4	4	3	5	4	5	3	4	5	5	4	4	4	5	4	5	5	78-152
Steven Young	Round 1	4	4	4	3	4	5	4	5	5	5	4	2	4	3	6	4	5	3	74
Scotland	Round 2	4	5	4	4	4	5	4	6	5	5	4	3	3	4	5	4	5	4	78-152
Frank Nobilo	Round 1	5	4	4	3	4	5	3	5	4	5	4	3	5	4	4	4	5	5	76
New Zealand	Round 2	4	5	4	3	4	4	5	4	4	4	4	3	3	6	6	5	5	5	77-153
Andrew Magee	Round 1	5	4	4	3	4	5	3	5	5	4	4	2	5	3	5	5	5	4	75
USA	Round 2	4	5	4	3	5	6	2	4	5	6	5	4	4	3	6	4	4	4	78-153
Russell Claydon	Round 1	5	4	4	3	5	4	3	4	4	5	3	3	5	3	6	5	4	4	74
England	Round 2	4	5	3	4	4	5	3	4	5	4	5	3	4	3	7	5	5	6	79-153
Mats Hallberg	Round 1	4	4	4	4	4	5	3	4	4	6	4	3	7	2	5	4	6	4	77
Sweden	Round 2	7	5	4	4	3	4	2	6	5	3	5	3	5	3	5	5	4	4	77-154
Daren Lee	Round 1	5	3	4	2	4	5	2	5	4	5	4	3	5	3	6	4	7	5	76
England	Round 2	6	4	4	3	4	5	4	4	4	4	5	3	5	4	6	4	5	4	78-154
Steven Armstrong	Round 1	5	5	4	3	4	4	3	5	5	4	5	3	4	3	7	4	4	4	76
England	Round 2	4	5	5	3	5	5	3	6	4	4	5	3	5	3	5	4	4	5	78-154
Robert Karlsson	Round 1	4	5	4	3	3	6	3	4	5	4	4	3	3	2	5	4	5	5	72
Sweden	Round 2	6	4	4	4	6	5	4	4	5	4	6	3	5	3	5	5	4	5	82-154
Ben Crenshaw	Round 1	4	4	5	3	4	4	3	4	5	4	6	3	4	2	5	5	6	5	76
USA	Round 2	5	5	4	3	5	6	3	3	4	4	5	4	4	3	7	4	5	4	78-154
Graham Spring	Round 1	5	4	4	2	4	5	3	4	3	4	5	3	4	4	6	5	5	4	74
Ireland	Round 2	5	5	4	3	6	5	4	5	5	5	4	4	4	3	6	4	4	4	80-154
Steve Alker	Round 1	5	4	4	3	4	4	3	3	4	5	5	4	4	2	5	4	5	5	73
New Zealand	Round 2	4	4	4	4	4	6	4	4	5	4	8	3	5	3	5	5	5	4	81-154
Mark Litton	Round 1	7	4	4	4	4	5	3	4	4	3	4	3	3	3	5	5	5	5	75
England	Round 2	4	4	4	3	4	7	3	4	4	5	5	3	5	3	6	5	6	5	80-155
Toru Suzuki	Round 1	5	5	5	2	4	4	3	4	4	5	4	3	5	3	5	5	5	7	78
Japan	Round 2	5	4	4	3	4	6	3	5	4	5	4	3	5	4	5	4	4	5	77-155
Gary Orr	Round 1	5	4	5	4	4	4	3	4	4	5	5	2	4	3	4	6	5	7	78
Scotland	Round 2	5	4	4	4	4	4	3	4	5	5	4	4	5	4	5	5	4	5	78-156
Bradley Dredge	Round 1	5	5	4	3	4	6	4	4	4	4	6	3	5	3	5	4	5	4	78
Wales	Round 2	5	4	4	3	6	6	2	4	5	4	5	3	5	3	5	5	4	5	78-156

HOLE		1	2	3	4	5	6	7	8	9	10	11	12	13	14	15	16	17	18	TOTAL
PAR		4	4	4	3	4	4	3	4	4	4	4	3	4	3	5	4	5	4	TOTAL
Stuart Appleby Australia	Round 1	5	4	4	3	5	4	3	4	6	4	4	4	4	3	5	3	6	5	76
	Round 2	5	4	5	4	4	5	3	4	4	4	4	3	4	6	5	5	4	7	80-156
Greig Hutcheon Scotland	Round 1	5	4	4	3	5	4	3	4	5	4	5	2	4	3	5	4	4	5	73
	Round 2	5	7	4	4	4	6	3	5	4	5	4	3	4	4	5	5	5	6	83-156
Scott Henderson Scotland	Round 1	4	4	5	3	6	5	3	4	4	4	5	4	6	3	5	4	4	4	77
	Round 2	4	4	4	3	4	6	4	4	3	5	4	5	5	4	6	5	5	5	80-157
Peter Hedblom Sweden	Round 1	4	5	3	3	4	4	3	5	5	4	4	3	6	3	6	4	5	5	76
	Round 2	5	4	4	3	5	4	4	5	4	5	5	4	5	3	6	4	6	6	82-158
Jeff Remesy France	Round 1	5	4	5	5	3	5	2	4	4	5	4	4	3	5	3	6	6	4	77
	Round 2	7	4	4	3	4	6	4	4	5	5	5	3	5	3	5	5	5	5	82-159
Miguel Angel Jimenez Spain	Round 1	4	4	4	3	4	5	3	4	4	4	4	4	4	5	4	5	4	4	73
	Round 2	5	6	4	3	5	5	3	5	4	4	5	3	4	3	7	4	3	5	78-DQ
Steve Elkington Australia	Round 1	4	5	5	3	4	4	3	6	5	5	4	3	4	3	5	4	4	4	75-WD
Francis Howley Ireland	Round 1	4	5	5	4	4	5	4	4	4	4	4	3	4	3	5	5	5	6	78-WD